Consider the Ravens

*A Story of God's Providence
from a Life of Uncertainties to a Life of Promise*

A Memoir

To
Lynne,

April 2022

I hope you enjoy my story ☺

God Bless!

Sandy Gamble John 3:16

Sandy Gamble

ISBN 978-1-63814-424-3 (Paperback)
ISBN 978-1-63814-425-0 (Hardcover)
ISBN 978-1-63814-426-7 (Digital)

Book cover design by Aaron Mondok

Covenant Books, Inc.
11661 Hwy 707
Murrells Inlet, SC 29576
www.covenantbooks.com

Consider the ravens, for they neither sow nor reap; they
have no storeroom nor barn, and yet God feeds them;
how much more valuable you are than the birds!

—Luke 12:24 (NASB)

Contents

Foreword

Most autobiographies are written by celebrities, statesmen, military heroes, business moguls, or those who triumphed over enormous personal challenges. Some authors are shamelessly self-aggrandizing. Others attempt to recount their life as objectively as possible. Some record their histories with bitter cynicism, while others present an idealized view of their life. This memoir doesn't fit any of those categories. Sandy Gamble is not a household name, nor does she wish it to be one. She is content to be an ordinary Christian living her life in faithful obscurity. She has no desire to make herself an admirable hero or an abused victim. Rather, she tells us her story to draw attention to the utter goodness of the Lord, who has exercised His merciful, sovereign care in every chapter of her life.

Sandy also writes because her unique childhood is such a beautiful exception to the ugly experiences of some who were brought up in group homes or with foster families. She recalls positively the care and nurture she received from those who provided guardianship when she needed it and encourages us to recognize that there are those who serve children with integrity and compassion. Further, she documents her sympathetic understanding of her biological parents, her affection for her grandparents, and her indebtedness to her "forever family" who not only demonstrated their love for her but also taught her of God's eternal love, expressed through Jesus Christ. Reading this account of one who was the recipient of such God-honoring care will be a special encouragement to those who are considering fostering or adopting.

Though I already knew Sandy as an exemplary member of the church I serve, reading the details of her early life and marriage caused me to laugh out loud, shed silent tears, and give thanks to the Lord, who planned every detail of "the days that were ordained for [her], when as yet there was not one of them" (Psalm 139:16). I believe it will do the same for every reader.

J. Todd Murray
Pastor of Family Ministries
Grace Immanuel Bible Church
Jupiter, Florida

Introduction

Everyone has a story. Events that involve people or places that, over time, help shape who we are. In 2017, my husband, Eric, and I revisited our home state of Ohio. We began to talk about my past one afternoon with our niece, Christina.

Christina, when she was younger, had heard my story of how the Summit County Children's Services (SCCS) helped me throughout my childhood. Christina later made a decision to pursue a career in social work. She told me that her previous knowledge of my time spent in foster care had sparked an interest in her to want to help and protect children and families in crisis.

She began her studies and received an undergraduate degree from Cedarville University. Then she went on to complete her master's degree in social work at the University of Akron. Before she graduated with her degree, she worked at SCCS doing case studies of people wanting to adopt or foster children.

During that summer visit, she asked me if I would like to go back to SCCS to see the home where I used to live. The house, which was no longer used, was set to be demolished later that fall. I was excited to revisit not only the property but also the memories of long ago.

Following that visit with Christina, the Lord put a desire in my heart to write. Not until then did I ever consider the significance of how sharing my story on a bigger scale could have an impact on others who may have traveled a similar road.

Over the past few years, I have gathered information, prayed, and processed over many memories. I have recalled things that I have not thought about in years. Many days as I sat typing, the tears would come, and then moments later I would find myself laughing.

I know this book is about so much more than my memories or events. It's about a journey—a journey that was ordained by God before I was even born. These words were written by me, but He is the author of this story. My prayer is that this book would glorify God and show that He can be trusted in all circumstances.

> For You formed my inward parts;
> You wove me in my mother's womb.
> I will give thanks to You, for I am fearfully and
> wonderfully made;
> Wonderful are Your works,
> And my soul knows it very well.
> My frame was not hidden from You,
> When I was made in secret,
> And skillfully wrought in the depths of the earth;
> Your eyes have seen my unformed substance;
> And in Your book were all written
> The days that were ordained for me,
> When as yet there was not one of them.
> (Ps. 139:13–16 NASB)

The Promise

My parents on their wedding day, August 1963

They were young when they got married. My father, although I don't know much about him, was tall and handsome with bright green eyes and dark brown hair. Most of the time he would grease and comb it back on the sides so it wouldn't move. Once in a while, a little curl would fall out of place and dangle on his forehead giving him that rustic, James Dean look. My mother was thin and frail with dark, almost black, haunting eyes. Her brown hair was about shoulder length. She would often wear it curled down around her face. Women didn't wear much makeup in the 1960s, although my mother did wear red lipstick. The color would contrast her eyes making them seem almost endless, like you could get lost in them. They were married in the summer of 1963. She was beautiful and quiet. He worked as a heavy-equipment operator; she was a homemaker. They did what they could, but money was tight.

There was talk of abuse and sadness in that first year of marriage. He drank a lot, and it got him into some serious trouble, which made the marriage all the more difficult. The sadness, heavy on my mother's heart, soon changed with news of a baby to be born in the spring. Only twenty-two, the thought of becoming a parent filled my mother with joy. The moments of uncertainty seemed to take a back seat to preparing for the new arrival. Plans were made to welcome this new little life soon to be born. Not knowing if the baby was a boy or a girl, Mother hoped in her heart for a girl. In the spring of 1965, her wish came true.

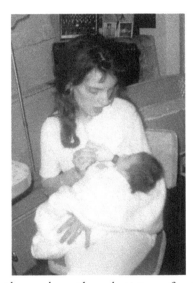

My mother and me, the only picture of us together

I was born in Akron, Ohio, to Phyllis and Elmer Cole. It was a happy day for my parents, full of excitement. A new baby, there is nothing like it. I had a head full of dark brown hair and green eyes, like my father's. My grandparents were thrilled. Maybe this would be a new start for Phyllis and Elmer. Maybe things would be better. Newborns bring out the hope in all of us. Unfortunately, that was all about to change. My story was about to begin, and no one saw the tragedy that would set the course of my life into motion and change the lives of so many others…but God did.

*****

It was evening; something wasn't right. My mother and my grandmother sat in the kitchen. As my mother put her head down on the table, she began to cry. She told my grandmother she was unhappy. Things hadn't changed with my father. If anything, they had gotten worse. The only reason she wanted to live was because of her new baby girl. My mother made my grandmother promise, "If anything happens to me, will you look after Sandy?"

"I promise," she replied.

That was the conversation that night. The next day, my mother was gone. As much as she wanted to be there for me, it wasn't meant to be.

I was only six weeks old. I'm not exactly sure of the cause of death. They say it was a postnatal complication from childbirth, most likely an infection. I always asked myself why nobody helped her. Maybe there was no money? Maybe no one knew the seriousness of her condition? I suppose that question will never be answered.

My father was left to care for me on his own but was sentenced to serve time in the Mansfield State Reformatory in January of 1966. He had been criminally charged with two counts of breaking and entering and one count of grand larceny. Based on concerns with my father, who now had a criminal and behavioral history, combined with the fact that he was unable to meet my basic needs, Summit County Children's Services (SCCS) was granted permanent custody of me in February of 1966. I never got to know my birth mother. My father, now serving time, was unable to care for me, so my grandparents assumed primary responsibility for my care, to which my father agreed.

In March of 1967, my father was released from Mansfield. He had expressed a desire to become part of my life again, so the agency developed a plan for me to remain with my grandparents and for my father to have opportunities to visit me. These visits were supposed to be monitored by SCCS, but this rule was not always followed.

He had come to the house one day wanting to take me. My grandparents wouldn't let him in the door. He was drunk and unruly. They were scared, so they called the police. I'm sure my father was angry, heartbroken with the loss of his wife, and frustrated because I had been taken away from him. He was in no condition to care for a baby; he couldn't take care of himself. I know my grandparents did the right thing. Because of the uncertainty of my safety, visitation was now to be provided at the SCCS. The last visit I had with my father was in December 1967. I wouldn't see him again for many years.

It wasn't easy on my grandmother. She had made a promise to my mother. It was a promise that she took very seriously. That promise would soon haunt her for many years to come. I was loved in the care of my grandparents. All of the uncertainties were behind me, so everyone thought.

Grandma's House

Grandma Cole holding me, standing in front of her house

The covered porch was the first thing you saw on the front of my Grandmother Beulah's tiny six-room house. A long winding dirt driveway looped around to the freestanding wood garage that stood next to the house. There was no indoor plumbing, which made trips to the outhouse a cold jaunt on those long Ohio winter nights.

Behind the house, near the outhouse, was a large garden, and beyond the garden were trees and fields. During the summer the fields were full of Queen Anne's lace. Large bright yellow and orange sunflowers lined the side yard, their heads tilted by the heaviness of the bloom. By late summer, the wildflowers from the field were almost as tall as me.

I had fun playing with my uncles, Billy and Bobby. They were my mom's brothers and also lived with my grandparents. They were older than me by about ten years. Despite the age difference, my uncles enjoyed having a "little sister" around. They kept me busy playing outside in the big field behind the house.

Uncle Bobby holding me in my grandmother's backyard

Me in the backyard

The summer that I remember was filled with all kinds of good things: fresh corn on the cob from the garden and red tomatoes that we used to make tomato and mayonnaise sandwiches on thick, soft white Wonder Bread. Slices of watermelon were sprinkled with salt and served ice cold. There was always something good to eat.

It was hot during the day but cooled off in the evening. We caught lightning bugs and put them in glass mason jars with holes poked in the lid so they wouldn't die. I watched them for only a while and then released them to fly away. I loved to watch them glow as I would send them flying like little twinkles of lights against the black night sky.

My Grandpa Floyd's rusty old red pickup truck sat abandoned at the back of the field by the garden. At times, I would climb up on the hood, which was warm from the afternoon sun, and play with the worn-out windshield wipers, moving them back and forth against the chipped and scratched glass. I always managed to get up onto the truck, but getting down was the tricky part. I would have to swing my leg around through the open driver's side window. Many times, I would get stuck with one leg in the window and one dangling off the side of the door. Holding on as tight as I could, I would eventually make my way into the cab of the truck where I had fun pushing the buttons on the AM radio and honking the horn to see if anyone noticed me.

Grandpa always wore his bib overalls, plaid shirt, and baseball hat. He had no teeth, which made it hard to understand him when he talked. Most people just smiled and shook their head in agreement with whatever he was trying to say. He was my dad's father, a widower. My grandmother, who was my mom's mother, was also widowed. Grandma's previous husband, Carlos, was killed in a car accident in Southern Ohio in 1960. Not many families can say the paternal grandfather and the maternal grandmother married, but mine can. I didn't understand it at the time, but they married in order to satisfy the state so that they could keep me. My grandmother was the only mommy I knew at the time, and she had no objection to me calling her mommy.

There were issues with my grandpa's past. Several of his children had been removed from his custody. SCCS had taken note of that while they reviewed where to place me. SCCS had to be sure I would be safe, so my grandparents were monitored to ensure that happened.

Although at the time I didn't know any different, my grandfather also struggled with being an alcoholic. He continued to deal with his own issues from his past while trying to do what he thought was best for me.

*****

I was somewhat of a tomboy, and I enjoyed being outside where I had the freedom to explore the property that surrounded Grandma's house. One afternoon I found myself playing with the stray dog that roamed our neighborhood. I had no idea where he lived and I don't recall his name. They say he liked to follow me. No matter where I went, that dog went too.

Behind the house were some recently used paint cans. Billy, my uncle, hadn't had a chance to get rid of them yet. No one was around when I happened upon those cans. If someone would have seen me, they surely would have hightailed it over to save that poor dog from what I was about to do.

Blue was the color, and there was just enough paint left to spark my whimsical, creative curiosity. By the time I was finished making my world a more "colorful" place, I had painted my dog! Not just a small area of the dog was covered but the whole pup. You can only imagine the horror when my uncle discovered what I had done. Billy spent many hours cleaning up my artwork, all the while lecturing me on how not to do that again. Finally, the poor thing came clean. I hear "Old Blue" eventually ran off and was never seen again. I can't say that I blame him.

I had a love for animals, and I would bring them home whenever I could. The stray cat that frequented the yard was no exception. Taking that cat by the tail, I would fling it over my shoulder and walk around with it. They say he never scratched me. Why he didn't is a mystery.

Grandmother's house seemed so small compared to the land around it. As you entered the house, the kitchen was to the right. You could only fit two people in that tiny kitchen at the same time. There was a small window at the end of the narrow room which looked out onto the front porch and driveway. In the dining room there was a large black wood-burning stove that took up a large portion of the space. I was always careful not to touch it. Flowered wallpaper covered half of the walls. The seams around the edges were yellow and just beginning to turn up from lack of adhesive. If coaxed, the whole sheet would come down with just one pull.

Getting to my bedroom required going through the dining room, through my grandmother's bedroom, and into a tiny room at the very back of the house. My room was very small, but I didn't know any different, and I didn't seem to care. I was happy. Late at night, I would wake up, needing to use the outhouse. Dreading having to leave my nice warm bed, I would hold it as long as possible. I remember one night I couldn't wait any longer. I jumped out of bed, practically tripping over my long nightgown. Throwing on my coat and boots, I rushed out the kitchen door. Fortunately, there was a light located on a utility pole that stood at the side of the yard. That light was a big help as it lit up the paved path so I could see where I was going. Making my way back to the house, I was now wide awake! It was always hard to fall back asleep after being jolted like that with the cold night air.

Entering the house, I passed through the dining room and the black wood-burning stove as I headed back to my room. I couldn't help but jump onto my grandparents' full-size bed. As I darted through the door, I threw off my coat, kicked off my boots, and plopped myself right on top of them, snuggling up under the covers. There was hardly room for two in that bed, let alone three, but they didn't mind. I loved the feeling of being warm and secure with them in that bed. I laid there listening as my grandmother's breathing slowed. It was soft and rhythmic. Grandpa had already drifted back to sleep. I could tell because he was gently snoring in his offbeat kind of way. I was happy, and I felt safe. I have many good memories of spending time with my grandparents; this night was just one of them.

Before Christmas, Grandma liked to decorate the house. I enjoyed helping her put ornaments on the little tabletop tree that she always set up in the living room. Once the tree was finished, we would spend the rest of the afternoon baking cookies, which was my favorite thing to do. My grandmother asked, "What would you like Santa to bring you?" My answer was like that of any other young girl my age. I wanted a guitar and an ironing board and a new pair of shoes. And that's just what I got!

My grandmother did the best she could caring for me. It wasn't easy. I was now three years old and I kept her busy. She loved me. Even if she hadn't made that promise to my mom, she wouldn't have done anything differently.

Grandma, Grandpa, Uncle Bobby, and me at Grandma's house before my mother's funeral

Me, less than a year old

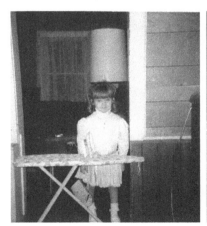

Grandma Cole's house. Me standing next to the wood-burning stove as I played with my ironing board.

My first birthday at my Grandma Cole's house, with my Uncle Bobby

The Accident

Me, age three or four

Times were different back in those days. No one wore seatbelts, and children were very rarely restrained in car seats. In the 1960s, car seats were created to contain children rather than protect them during a crash. Needless to say, I was not in one. Our neighbor, a nice black lady, had a car, and Grandma and I, on occasion, would tag along with her to the store.

She was my friend. Many times, I would make my way to her house by cutting through her garden at the side yard. During the summer I enjoyed picking blackberries as I walked along. Now that it was fall, the corn had been harvested and the stalks that were left were brown and limp from the cooler weather. The fields had some pumpkins in them now.

When I visited her, she always greeted me with a smile and invited me in. Quite often, she offered me cookies that she had recently baked. After she poured me a glass of milk, she placed a few cookies on my napkin. I liked to sit and talk with her while she finished whatever chore she had been working on. We both enjoyed the same kind of cookies except when she made oatmeal raisin. I always picked the raisins out and just ate the cookie part.

It was a cool fall day in October of 1968. Grandpa had not come home the night before. Grandma was worried. She knew Grandpa had been out drinking. She was concerned, not only for his safety but that his behavior would jeopardize our family. She didn't want any more trouble, and she was determined to find him and bring him home before anything bad happened. Grandma sat in the front while our neighbor drove. As the ladies discussed where to look first, I became bored and restless. And since I was an energetic three-year-old, I began jumping and playing in the back seat. Grandma had turned around several times scolding me to try and get me to sit still, but I was having such a good time I paid no attention to her.

And then it happened.

Jolted and thrown into the back of the seat in front of me, my head hit the side window, pain shot through my body like I had never felt before. The car finally came to a stop; I don't know how long I was unconscious.

While turning onto the main street outside of our neighborhood, our neighbor hadn't seen the car coming. As the two cars collided, time seemed to stand still. When I came to, a group of people had surrounded the car. I was still in the back, half on the floor and half on the seat. My grandmother was still in the seat in front of me, but she wasn't moving.

I could hear muffled voices talking to me. They were trying to get me out of the car. Dazed and trembling, I slid across the vinyl seat toward the driver's side. I saw our neighbor lying on the ground. I collapsed into the arms of a man wearing white. He scooped me up in his arms. To me, he seemed very tall.

As I was lifted up, I could see the wreckage all around me. My friend, our neighbor, was lying on the ground and she was bleeding; I had never seen so much blood. I was placed on a long flat board as they were careful not to move me unless they had to. I was quickly whisked away to a waiting ambulance. I was scared. What happened?

Where are you taking me? Where is my grandmother? Why do I hurt so much?

The ambulance was loud. The tall person who had lifted me out of the car was now looking into my eyes with a small flashlight, first the right eye and then the left. As I looked up at him, he smiled and asked, "What's your name?" I mumbled, but before the words even left my mouth, he had turned to grab something from his bag. "You're going to be okay. We are going to take good care of you." As I looked around at the back of the ambulance, I noticed that it wasn't very big. Slowly my vision began to narrow, with blackness coming in on both sides.

The hospital room had several beds. Mine was located next to the door that led to the bustling hallway. Everyone was wearing white, and it smelled funny. There was a window beside the door next to my bed. The nurses would peek through the window from time to time to check on me. I could see them looking, but I pretended I was asleep. I couldn't go anywhere; my bed was high with metal rails on both sides so I couldn't roll out. I didn't feel like getting up anyway. I had sustained head and collar bone fractures, and I had a large gash over my right eye that had required several stitches. Despite what had happened, my family was told that I was going to be okay.

There was one other little girl in the bed to the far side of the room. I didn't know her. She was quiet and just looked at me; she wasn't there long, and I suppose she went home. I recall being in that room for many days. To me it seemed like a very long time.

Relatives came to visit and brought me toys and things to do while I was recovering. I remember getting an Etch A Sketch, which I would pick up and play with during those in-between times when my head wasn't hurting, and a black stuffed poodle with an AM radio in its tummy. I was told my grandmother was going to be okay. She had been taken to a different hospital since she had sustained more significant injuries that required a long recovery period. My grandfather had regretted his decision that he had made that night when he didn't come home. He had been found and told of the accident. He was not able to care for me during my recovery time. Little did I know how the accident would impact my life...things were again about to change.

❀ Buttermilk

Me with my two cousins, Kenny and Terry

After two weeks in the hospital, I was discharged but was not able to live with my grandparents while my grandmother recovered from the accident. My grandfather, still struggling with his alcoholism, was not permitted to care for me. My father had not been a part of my life for some time, so the Summit County Children's Services (SCCS) placed me with the next available family members—my maternal Uncle Gary and Aunt Carol and their two sons, my cousins, Kenny and Terry.

Buttermilk—I loved it. My aunt always got the real buttermilk, the one that was made locally. It was the best kind with chunks of real butter in it. Late at night I would get out of my bed and sneak into the kitchen when I thought no one was watching. I would drink that cold wonderful buttermilk right out of the carton. I tried my best to be stealthy, but my aunt always seemed to hear me getting into the refrigerator. One night, she went to the kitchen, knowing all along what I was doing. At four years old, I thought no one could see me if I closed my eyes tightly enough. That was my plan. It was dark, so how could anyone spot me?

As I sat there, curled up on the floor against the cupboard with my knees against my chest, making myself as small as I could so I wouldn't be detected, Aunt Carol made her way around the kitchen, careful not to step on me. She reached around and did the one thing I hadn't thought of—she opened the refrigerator door.

The light coming from inside the refrigerator illuminated the whole kitchen like I was on a stage getting ready to perform. My carefully planned midnight excursion had been foiled. As I waited for the moment of reckoning, Aunt Carol, to my surprise, closed the refrigerator, walked past me, and shuffled down the hall to her bedroom and closed the door. It was amazing. This was astonishing proof that I had the superpower of invisibility. I decided I had pushed the limit as far as I dare. As I picked myself up off the floor, I too quietly shuffled down the hall to my room and closed the door.

I pulled the covers up around my chin. As I lay there, I thought to myself how wonderful it was that I could get away with something so daring. So with a satisfying feeling of accomplishment, a milk mustache on my face, and my belly full of buttermilk, I was soon fast asleep.

The next morning, I was expected to eat my breakfast. But I refused. I had developed a rebellious habit of not wanting to eat. Every morning at breakfast and every night during dinner I would scream and fight. The battle was almost too much for my aunt and uncle to handle. It was a difficult time for Kenny and Terry as well. They were kids themselves and couldn't understand what was happening. When I came to live with them, I turned their once uneventful lives upside down.

My aunt became more worried about my health. As we walked out to the road with my cousins so they could catch the bus, she looked at me and told me she loved me and she wished I would eat my breakfast. Refusing food became an ongoing battle. In my mind, as a young child, I couldn't explain or understand the reason why I wasn't happy. There had been some major changes in my life that clearly had an effect on me. I continued to be angry and stubborn. No one could make me eat. I was determined to win.

In my rebellion, I would yell and protest anytime I was told what to do. My aunt was so beside herself that she came up with the idea of tape recording one of my tantrums. Hearing my voice on the tape as it was played back only made matters worse. I would shout at her to turn it off, to which she replied, "This is what you sound like!"

Anger continued to be a big part of my life. I became destructive. I would destroy my toys and dolls. One afternoon I got a hold of a pair of scissors and cut up the pretty comforter that my aunt had bought for my bed.

The struggle continued. No matter what my aunt did, I wasn't happy. One day, Aunt Carol took Kenny, Terry, and me shopping. She let each of us pick out a toy. My cousins went for the trucks and cars. I wanted a doll. Thinking we were all happy with our choices, she purchased the toys and we got in the car and went home. It wasn't long after we got home that I again became angry with the toy I had picked out. I broke my toy, and, in a rage, I screamed that I wanted a truck like my cousins had.

It seemed that it didn't matter how hard Aunt Carol and Uncle Gary tried, I wanted to do things my way, especially when it came to mealtime. I had been through a lot already at the age of four, and food was the one thing that I could control. I probably knew refusing food at mealtime would make my aunt and uncle upset and that's just what I intended to do.

The psychologist that I had been meeting with told Aunt Carol that the reason I was so angry was probably because I was no longer living with my grandmother. I had been taken away from the only home I ever knew. I couldn't go back to live with my grandparents. The state had been monitoring my grandpa and decided that a different relative would be a better choice.

I would see my grandmother occasionally when Aunt Carol took me to her house for a visit. When it was time to go home with Aunt Carol, I fought the fact that I no longer lived with Grandma. Hunger strikes, sneaking food in the middle of the night, and lashing out in fits of rage and anger became the way I dealt with my situation.

*Me standing in Grandma's
tiny kitchen*

Kenny, Bobby, Terry, and me

It was lunchtime; my cousins were outside playing. As I sat in the kitchen with a plate full of food in front of me, I was determined. I watched my cousins through the glass sliding door and began contemplating my next move. Then, unexpectedly, Aunt Carol left the room. Did she understand what she had done, leaving me to find a way out of this situation I was in? Without a second thought, I opened the kitchen drawer where I was sitting and proceeded to scrape the entire contents of my plate into it, closing it slowly so as not to make a sound. Oh, the pride I felt as I had successfully and carefully executed my plan to outsmart the food police.

Upon returning to the kitchen, she seemed impressed with the way I had devoured everything on my plate. "You must be anxious to go out and play," she said. I was excused from the table, so I headed out to play as quickly as I could. I was so proud that I had successfully fooled everyone. I ran to greet my cousins, and I put the whole incident out of my mind, until...

The drawer I chose was not often used, so it was at least a week before my deception was discovered. Standing in the corner of my purple-painted bedroom on a regular basis became the norm for me. I would stand in my room until it got dark, and then I was told it was time for bed. It was a hard time for me. I didn't understand why it was such a big deal that I didn't want to eat. I didn't understand why I was doing it and was sad because it seemed I was always in trouble. Clearly I was developing some serious issues and needed help. I didn't like standing in the corner of my dark room. Why was this happening? Aunt Carol and Uncle Gary were running out of ideas.

Aunt Carol was so concerned about my eating habits that she took me to see the doctor at SCCS. The visits to the doctors did no good. I continued to refuse to eat. During one of my many visits to see the physician and after a thorough examination, he explained to my aunt that I was getting dehydrated and I needed to change my behavior, and soon. Looking me square in the eye, he reprimanded me, saying, "Sandy, you need to start eating. You will make yourself sick!" Without hesitation, I raised my hand and, with a right hook that would make any boxer proud, I flung my hand around and smacked the doctor right across his face.

Shocked by the reality of being so caught off guard, he flinched backward and gasped. As he put his hand on his face, he stared at me. I had succeeded, I had made my point, and I wasn't going to listen to him anymore. Oh, the look of terror on my aunt's face! She was so embarrassed. She quickly apologized, gathered my things and her purse, and clutched my hand in hers as we exited the office.

She never said a word as she opened the door so I could get into the back seat of the car. The silence we shared during that long drive let me know that as soon as we got home I would be visiting the corner of my purple bedroom once again.

*****

Some memories of life with my aunt and uncle are vague while others remain very clear. Certain things like smells or tastes can spark long-forgotten memories. Aunt Carol had a bottle of hand lotion that always sat on the counter near the sink in the kitchen. From time to time my aunt would squirt a small amount into my palm. I can remember breathing in deeply the cherry almond scent before rubbing it all over my hands. It wasn't until years later that the smell of Jergens hand lotion caused me to recall this memory.

M&M's were also a memory that I have from my time at my aunt's house. She kept a bowl of plain M&M's on the back of the toilet in the bathroom located across the hall from my bedroom.

The bowl rested on a colorful fuzzy tank cover that also came with a matching seat cover and rug. Each time I visited the restroom, I would reach around and grab as much as I could of those sweet colorful pieces of happiness, putting the whole handful into my mouth at once. I have to say, it was a highlight of my trips to use the bathroom. Why were they there? I don't know, but it did make my potty time more enjoyable!

I have memories of dressing up with my cousins and going trick-or-treating for Halloween and of playing all day with Mary, the little girl that lived in the house behind ours. When I did eat, it was a grilled cheese sandwich that I enjoyed dipping into a bowl of piping hot tomato soup. I remember so much, but why? Why did God allow all these memories to stay with me?

Cambridge

Me, age three or four

Aunt Carol had a relative that owned land in Cambridge, Ohio. They had a large property where they raised dairy cows. During the summers, we often visited the old farm. I always looked forward to spending time at the house, but enduring the long car ride to get there was another story.

The two-lane country road was long. Packed into the family car, I sat in the back seat between my two cousins, Kenny and Terry. The windows were down, and the dust that kicked up as we traveled swirled around inside and then exited as quickly as it came. Driving maybe a little too fast, my uncle made his way with us in tow.

Adjusting the radio so she could talk, Aunt Carol, who was sitting next to my uncle, kept telling him to slow down, which he chose to ignore as he drove faster. Knowing all along what he was doing, he quickly glanced at me from the rearview mirror. His eye caught mine, shooting me one of his crooked half grins. I quickly smiled back. Driving with just his wrist over the steering wheel, he kept his left arm dangling out the driver's side window, moving his hand up and down as if pretending it was an airplane. As I watched him enjoying teasing my aunt, his bright blue eyes darted to the left and then the right as he shifted the well-worn toothpick from side to side in his mouth. I couldn't help but notice how his thick, dark sideburns faded into his windblown hair. My aunt always looked nice with her shoulder-length black hair tied neatly in a ponytail with a ribbon.

Cornfields lined the left side of the road. Trying to count them was just about impossible since we were moving so fast. Occasionally, the fields were interrupted by pastures scattered with black-and-white dairy cows. The smell in the air was mostly of hay and manure. Once in a while, my cousins would grab their noses and make comments on how the other one stunk, poking at each other with me trying to keep peace as I sat between them. We were almost there, but the car ride seemed to take forever.

It was hot, midsummer. The only breeze was the one we enjoyed while the car was moving. Sitting next to two sweaty boys was the last thing I wanted to do. Brushing my hair out of my eyes, I could see the big red barn just around the corner. Cambridge lies in southeastern Ohio, in the Appalachian Plateau of the Appalachian Mountains. The beautiful hills all around were calling to me to come and explore. As I sat daydreaming about what I would do first, we slowed down and turned into the wide dirt driveway that separated the barn from the house. Pushing my cousin to hurry him out of the way, I couldn't get out of the car fast enough.

The white farmhouse was quite old. As I got closer, I could see the white paint was beginning to peel off the wooden slats. It had a long porch on the front where several rocking chairs gently moved in the hot summer breeze. No one ever used the front door; the kitchen was located in the back. We quickly grabbed our stuff and made our way around to the rickety screen door. Not realizing how light it was, I gave it a good tug. It opened so quickly I almost lost my footing. As I entered the kitchen, it slammed shut behind me just as quickly as it had opened.

The smell of sweet corn cooking in a big pot on the stove filled the air. The tall windows that towered on one wall of the small room had gathered condensation from the pot boiling on the stove. The smell of cornbread, which was always baked in a cast-iron pan, was coming from the oven.

Running up the stairs, I entered the big room at the top of the house. It was filled with all kinds of things no one used anymore. I always enjoyed looking at all of the old, dusty stuff. As I walked into the room, a black leather travel trunk caught my eye. I placed my things next to it and gave it a good kick with my red tennis shoe. I was tempted to open it and paused for a few minutes to examine its well-worn exterior. Curious to know what treasures it held, I used both hands to lift the lid. Try as I might, I couldn't get it open. Giving up, I ran down the long flight of wooden stairs and out the kitchen door, not caring if it slammed.

Running across the driveway, I entered the barn. It was my favorite place. A few cows were in their stalls, and the smell of manure and hay filled the air. Finding my way around the stalls, I greeted each animal. I noticed one of the cows was much bigger than the others. Not giving it a second thought, I ran out the door and scurried up the hill that backed up to the kitchen door. As I ran, I stopped only once because I was out of breath. Finally reaching the top of the hill, I turned to see all that was around me.

The sun was beginning to set, the lightning bugs were coming out, and the air felt a little cooler. I felt at peace, like the world was all mine to explore. Visiting Cambridge was different from where I now lived—not a soul for miles, lots of room to run, and animals, which I loved.

During dinner I picked at my food, as usual. I just sat there looking at everyone else, still refusing to eat. After dinner it was time for bed. As I headed up the stairs, I moved a little slower than I did earlier that day. I was tired. Digging through my bag, I found my toothbrush. There was only one bathroom in the old farmhouse. Finally, it was my turn. My cousins were sharing the room across the hall from the bathroom. I could see them through the cracked door. They were throwing pillows at each other and laughing. I didn't want to get involved in a pillow fight since they were much bigger than me and I would probably get hurt. Instead, I was looking forward to the fun we would have tomorrow playing in the cornfields. I was usually better at hiding than they were.

After I closed the bathroom door, I stepped up to the sink and used the stool to reach the spigots. There was only one sink and it was old. Some of the porcelain had chipped off the bottom. The faucet handles were white, one had an *H* on the top and the other had a *C*. As I stood there brushing my teeth, I noticed a daddy longlegs spider crawling across the white-and-black tile floor. *Good thing my cousins didn't see you*, I thought. And good for me too! I knew they would use the poor thing to scare me, and I wasn't up for that. I finished brushing my teeth and walked back to the room where I would sleep. My cousins were now quiet. The only noise upstairs in the house was the floorboards that creaked as I walked.

Sounds in the country were much different than the neighborhoods I had lived in. The big tall windows in my room were open, letting in a breeze. Looking through them, I could see as far as the surrounding hills would let me. The glass in the window had a wave in it that I found myself studying. It was very old, and some of the panes had small cracks. As the sun was setting over the cornfields, I could hear the katydids as they chirped in the night air. They seemed to say, "Katy did, Katy didn't, Katy did, Katy didn't." There were cows mooing in the distance and an occasional car passing by on the dirt road in front of the house.

As the adults were talking down in the kitchen, I crawled into the sleeping bag that I had brought with me. I stared at the night light on the wall to my right. It was shaped like a horseshoe, and it gave a soft glow to the room that left shadows on the walls. Sleepy, I thought to myself, *I can't wait until morning; tomorrow is going to be a fun day!*

*****

The sun was coming up when I heard the first rooster crow. Tucked snuggly in my sleeping bag, I studied the big black travel trunk beside me, counting all the round gold rivets that framed the outside.

Voices were coming from downstairs, and the smell of bacon was filling the air. I quickly dressed, put on my red tennis shoes, and made my way down the stairs. Not really wanting to eat, I headed outside to play. Up over the hill was an old graveyard. The last time we came for a visit my cousins had taken me with them to explore it. Now that I was a year older, I wanted to see it for myself. It wasn't far from the house—just up the hill. Running as fast as I could, it didn't take long for me to reach it.

Some of the gravestones had fallen over, some were cracked, and some had vines and tall grass growing around them like they had been there for a long time. A wrought iron fence encompassed the group of about twenty plots. Some of the graves had smaller fences just around them. I always wondered why. Was that to keep someone out or to keep someone in? A canopy of trees covered the area, which made it cooler as the day began to heat up. It was a quiet place. Birds were about the only thing you could hear except for an occasional rooster crowing off in the distance.

As I walked around, I thought about how much more exciting it was the last time I came with my cousins. Since they could read and I couldn't, they would read the head stones while making up stories just to frighten me. They would chase me around while I squealed with the excitement of being scared. Since I was by myself this time, my mind began to wander with the thought of the scary stories my cousins had told the year before. I began to hum a little song—nananna. I once heard that humming keeps the monsters away. Although I was by myself, it was morning, and I knew I was safe—no monsters could get me. After all, everyone knows that monsters only come out at night.

My cousins, Kenny and Terry, spent a lot of time with me. They did the best they could to make me happy, but I continued to want things my way. At least when we were in Cambridge, we all had space to roam and explore. I loved the farm and really didn't want to go back to my aunt and uncle's house.

I walked back the way I came in through the gate and back toward the top of the hill. As I walked through the tall grass, small bugs flew up and got in my face. I brushed the bugs out of my bangs and found a clearing where I could sit. I could see my uncle and a few people standing in the dirt driveway on the far side of the house. I could see my cousins heading down the road. I could tell they were up to no good, so this time, I was glad I wasn't with them.

Walking back down the hill, I heard commotion in the barn. I was curious and hurried to see what was going on. Men in overalls were standing next to one of the stalls. I squeezed past them to see what was causing all the excitement. My uncle saw me come in and quickly escorted me back out to the dirt driveway. "Not now, Sandy," he said. Puzzled, I skipped over to the steps on the front porch of the farmhouse. I sat and rocked in one of the rocking chairs, watching and waiting.

I could hear them talking but didn't understand what was being said. After what seemed like a long time to me, I decided to find out on my own and began walking toward the barn. My uncle saw me coming; he was more receptive to me this time around. Taking my hand, he walked me over to the stall with the cow, the one I had noticed the day before, the one that was bigger than the others. She was now lying down. Next to her was a newborn calf. As the cow struggled, she soon got to her feet. The calf was so small. He was brown with a white patch on his nose. Taking his time, he leaned forward on his knees. His back legs stretched out to help balance the weight of his hind quarters as he pushed himself up.

The men standing around gave a celebratory cheer. My uncle looked at me and smiled with his crooked grin, to which I smiled back. How amazing, how wonderful! This was the best trip to Cambridge ever! I believe we remember special moments, important things that happen in our lives, and this was one of those moments I will never forget.

*****

Our visit to Cambridge seemed to go so fast. I was disappointed to have to leave. I never wanted to say goodbye to the animals. I knew I would miss the adventures I had each day exploring the barn and the cornfields.

Throwing my sleeping bag into the trunk, I climbed into the back seat of the car and took my place between my two cousins. It was now time to leave and head back to my aunt and uncle's house. As my uncle backed out of the dirt driveway, I glanced over at the house and barn, and a sense of sadness came over me. I didn't know it at the time, but it would be many years before I would go back to visit the farm I loved so much. Settling into one place wasn't going to happen for me.

I continued to struggle with my eating disorder and behavioral issues. My aunt and uncle found it very difficult to manage me. In November of 1970, when I was five years old, my social worker intervened and notified my doctor that I was not doing well. My social worker took me to the children's home clinic where I was to receive treatment and monitoring because I was losing too much weight.

The medical clinic was located close to the dental clinic inside of a large brick building that also housed offices for the Summit County Children's Services. Only children who were very sick got to go there. I was admitted and given a bed with crisp white sheets. The nurses, all in white with funny hats on their perfectly groomed hair, were all behind a glass wall, a nurse's station. They came in and out from behind the wall from time to time to check on me.

In the early morning, while it was still dark, the smell of coffee filled the room; it was a comforting aroma, not one I smelled very often. There were other beds in the room, but they were empty. I was the only one, so of course I got special treatment. I didn't have to share the attention with anyone else. My condition was pretty serious, so I remained in the medical clinic for several weeks.

The nurses were very loving and seemed to really enjoy what they did. It was a comforting feeling waking up in that place. It left such an impression on me that I really didn't mind if I got sick again and had to go back. After that, every time I smelled coffee it would remind me of the kind nurses dressed in white in the little room behind the glass.

After my two weeks' stay in the clinic, I was not permitted to return to my aunt and uncle's house because I needed to complete my treatment and counseling. By this time, my father had remarried and SCCS had no further contact with him. I soon found myself relocating again, this time to a place I had never been.

The Red Balloon

My feet went as far as the top of the vinyl back seat. The car was huge, and I was the only one in it except for the lady driver. It was a cool sunny day, and I enjoyed the beautiful red balloon I had been given. There was a song that caught my attention playing on the car radio. The words and melody somehow stayed with me. As I look back on it now, the lyrics of the song, "Seattle," seem to be hauntingly appropriate for what was about to come.

The song spoke of a child full of dreams and laughter who had to leave his home and loved ones. It spoke of green hills and blue skies, fears, tears, and uncertainties. It spoke of prayer and the hope that someday someone warm and sweet and kind would be waiting there for him. But no one really knows what the future holds, do they?

The car ride wasn't very long, so I played with my balloon and hummed to the music until the car stopped. When the lady who had been driving opened the door to let me out of the back seat, I stepped out onto the sidewalk and realized we were parked on a hill.

The street was narrow and was lined with two-story houses on both sides. The houses were tall and seemed to tower high above me, going on forever up into the sky. There were sidewalks and big trees that were along both sides of the road. When you're five years old and only forty inches tall, the world seems like a much bigger place.

As we approached the house, which was named Corner House, a cold breeze touched my face. My blond hair danced up off my shoulders and onto my back. It was a Monday morning, just before Thanksgiving, and the day was beautiful. As I walked along the sidewalk, my balloon brushed a low branch on one of the trees and popped. Startled, I was left with nothing but the lifeless red balloon tied to the string.

Climbing up the large stone steps to the house was challenging for me because I was so small. The big white door was quickly opened to reveal a bustling room full of girls giggling and running around. *Sesame Street* was playing on the large TV in the middle of the living room, and a tall dark-haired woman was setting the table in the dining room to the left. To the right was a long wood ornate staircase that went up to the second floor where there were several bedrooms.

I watched as the two women greeted each other. Some of the girls who were running around stopped to look my way. They seemed to be just as curious about me as I was about them. Formal introductions now over, I made my way up the tall wooden staircase hand in hand with the dark-haired lady that had been in the dining room. Each wooden step seemed to squeak as we shifted our weight. Two of the rooms had bunk beds. I was told the one with the pink sheets was mine. As I placed my belongings on the bottom bed, I looked around the room. It had old faded wallpaper, which brought back memories of my grandmother's dining room with the black wood-burning stove. The ceiling was high, and a little light hung in the center. It was getting dark, and the light was too dim to be of any use. The room had a musty smell that was slowly being overpowered by the smell of the meal cooking in the kitchen downstairs.

I didn't know how long I would have to stay at this place, but I wasn't afraid. Somehow, I knew this was now going to be my home. Looking down at my hand, I had forgotten I was holding the popped balloon with the string still attached. I walked over and tossed it into the trash can located by the only window at the far side of the room.

As I looked down to the street below, the lady that had driven me was digging through her purse to find her keys. She quickly unlocked the door to her car and got in. Glancing back at the house, her eyes made their way up to the second-floor window. I smiled and waved. She waved back, and then in a minute, she was gone. Somewhere in my little five-year-old mind I knew she wasn't coming back for me. As the dark-haired lady turned to walk out of the room, she motioned for me to follow her as she headed back toward the stairs. Dinner was ready. *Oh no*, I thought, *not again*.

I remained at Corner House for several weeks, until mid December. My next place of residence was just down the hill. My aunt and uncle wished for me to return to their home and primary care. However, I still needed to continue my treatment, so custody was denied. I was unable to return to my natural family since I still needed help for my disorder. At only five years old, I was dealing with some serious health and mental issues. Cottages were available through SCCS to house children in need of continued treatment and counseling. This was to be the next step for me.

Cole Cottage

The Summit County Children's Home
built around 1910
(Picture courtesy of Summit County Children Services)

The children's home was established in the early twentieth century, and it sheltered thousands of the county's dependent children. Its name was later changed to Summit County Children's Services. The institution is located on South Arlington Street in the extreme southeast corner of Akron, Ohio. It was a stately old brick building with beautiful large trees and a green lawn that was bordered by a short stone wall.

They named it after me—Cole Cottage—or at least at that time I thought they did. Cole Cottage was named for Mary Price Cole. She was a former helper and nurse's aide in the children's home clinic during the 1930s. In 1968, agency foster homes were established in newly acquired cottages on Clark Street, next to the institution. These cottages provided a practical option to house some of the children who were in the agency's system. The board of directors opened the first two agency foster homes in 1969, one for boys and one for girls and each staffed with a house mother.

Six little girls soon occupied Cole Cottage; it was the first house at the top of a small hill. The house had three bedrooms. Two of the bedrooms contained three little beds, one on each side and one in the middle. There were three small dressers, one at the foot of each bed, and three narrow closets. We didn't have many clothes or belongings, so we didn't really need much room for storage.

The third bedroom was the housemother's room. Her door was usually closed, except for one time it was left open and my curiosity got the best of me. No one was around, so I peeked around the corner. It was a normal room. A bed, a lamp, and clothes strewn here and there, but what caught my eye was something I had never seen before: a glass sitting on the nightstand which contained an odd-shaped item. At a closer look, the glass was half full of water and what looked like teeth were submerged in the cloudy liquid.

What in the world had I gotten myself into? My housemother quickly shooed me out of her private quarters and told me to go play. I couldn't help but wonder how she was going to eat dinner that night if her teeth were in a glass beside her bed?! Dinner that evening was interesting, to say the least. All six of us girls and the housemother sat together in the dining room at the large table that was central to the middle of the house. I'm sure she caught me looking at her several times as I watched in anticipation for something, anything, to fall out of her mouth and plop onto the dinner plate in front of her. To my surprise, she continued to enjoy her meal while juggling the cares of getting all six of us five-year-olds to eat.

*****

SCCS tried to keep life at Cole Cottage as normal as they could for all of us. There were five other girls in the house, so I always had someone to play with. There was a large white toy box located under the window in the large playroom by the side door. The toy box was big enough to fit any one of us girls inside. Once, we took all the toys out of it just to see if we could. People from the community would be generous and donate toys so we had toys to play with. On the wall adjacent to the toy box hung a clock in the shape of a cat. It was black and had white and black eyes and a long tail that would move as it would ticktock the day away. At times, I was certain the eyes followed me around the room as if they were watching me.

In the basement hung swings attached to the wood rafters. What fun we had swinging all year round no matter what the weather was like. The backyard of Cole Cottage was beautiful—large shade trees and toys which were strewn here and there. There was a fence that divided the property from the adjoining houses. There were also swings in the yard that allowed me to swing so high that at times I imagined myself jumping right over the big trees close by. All of us girls enjoyed playing together each day in that yard during the warmer months.

The living room had a small TV. We watched it each night after dinner and only if our homework was done. Sunday night was our favorite. *The Wonderful World of Disney* came on at seven. Tinker Bell would fly out from behind the castle, wave her magic wand, and the show would begin.

During the show, each girl got a big bowl of ice cream. My favorite was tin roof sundae. It was full of peanuts. I was careful to save the nuts so I could eat them last after my ice cream was gone. After the show was over, we were sent to our rooms to brush our teeth. Then off to bed and lights out. After the customary nighttime talking and giggles, the house grew quiet, and the only sound in the house was the ticking of the cat clock that hung in the playroom, keeping watch over our little house while we slept.

*****

The holidays were an exciting time at Cole Cottage. People from the community would visit or we would go places where there would be special activities. I especially enjoyed Easter egg hunts at the local park. Before Christmas, volunteers would help us make decorations to put on our Christmas tree. Relatives of the girls who lived with me in the cottage would spend time with us. They would bring gifts. Sometimes I got jealous of the new toys the other girls received.

Another visitor we had was a funny little man with suspenders and a colorful, tall hat. He entered the side door of the house and quickly got our attention, not only by what he had on but by the way he mesmerized us with his magical tricks. All of us girls were so intrigued with how quickly he could make a quarter disappear and then magically pull it from behind one of the girl's ears. All of us would squeal and ask what else he could do.

He presented us with an invisible red ball and a small brown paper bag. How did we know it was invisible? We knew because we couldn't see it. How did we know it was red? We knew because he told us so. Each child got a turn throwing the pretend ball up in the air. Each time he would swirl around the room as if to imply the throw was a little bit off the mark. Each time the bag would snap as if something had landed inside of it. Needless to say, we were all amazed and begged him to do it again, to which he was happy to comply.

*****

Aunt Carol and Uncle Gary had a difficult time accepting the fact that I was now in the custody of the state and no longer able to live with them. Uncle Gary refused to come to visit me. It was too hard on him. He knew he would not be able to take me back to his home and that was very difficult for him. Aunt Carol would usually come by herself. At the end of our visit, we would have to say good-bye. I never understood why I wasn't allowed to go home with her.

One Sunday afternoon as visitors were leaving, after a long visit from one of the local churches, I helped place all of the toys we had played with back into the large white toy box that sat under the window in the playroom. The girls all decided to go down into the basement to play. It had been raining all day, and being cooped up in the house had made everyone antsy.

I, for some reason, didn't want to join them. The sun was coming out from behind the dark clouds, but it was still too wet to go outside. I stood at the back door of the cottage and looked out the window. A rainbow had formed, and the sky was full of color. Leaning my back against the door frame, I slowly slid down until I was seated as close to the screen door as I could go. Even though the sounds from the basement indicated the girls were having a good time, I wasn't interested in joining them. It seemed I would often find myself sitting alone…lost in my thoughts.

The beauty of the rainbow drew me in. I must have sat there for a while as I tried to name all the colors I could see. Before I realized it, dinner was ready. All the girls came running up the stairs to wash their hands and take their seats at the table. When I think back on those times I spent at the children's home, I didn't always feel bad about my situation. In fact, I have good memories. I didn't understand a lot of what was happening. God had a plan. He was in control. I just didn't know it yet.

Cole Cottage; you can barely read the "Cole Cottage" sign located by the railing.

The backyard of Cole Cottage. I took these pictures the day we went on the tour with Christina, August 2017.

Truancy

Kindergarten picture when I lived at Cole
Cottage and attended Mason School

Mason School sat up on the hill, past the street lined with big trees and sidewalks where I once lived. All the children who were wards of the children's home walked to school together. The sidewalk connected to the walkway that was just outside the front door of Cole Cottage. We had fun as we giggled and played along our thirty-minute walk down the road and up the hill.

One winter morning, the snow was falling so fast it made it difficult to see as all of us girls began our walk. As I started out the door with the other children, I watched the wind blow the tops of the leafless trees that surrounded the backyard of the cottage. They bent back and forth as if they were waving to me. I was almost out of sight of Cole Cottage when I heard the house mother call my name from the front of the house. I was smaller than most of the children and had lagged behind as they walked, so she made me come back inside for fear I would get separated from the group.

The next day the snow covered the front of the house so that we couldn't get out when we opened the door. We had never seen such snow. It was beautiful. That day, school was called off, so all of us girls crowded around the window in the living room to watch as the fluffy white snowflakes fell to the ground.

The icicles that formed on the roof of the house hung over the window like giant daggers, each one a different size and each one with a tiny point at the end that would continually drip water as the day got warmer. When the sun finally came out, the icicles began to melt faster, sparkling in the sunlight as they began to disappear from the heat of the day.

Rain or snow, we had to walk to school. Each morning we got dressed and had breakfast together at the large table. The smell of CoCo Wheats filled the air. I never really ate much, but at the age of five, I was definitely in love with chocolate. If they could get me to eat a bowl of the creamy hot cereal that tasted like cocoa, they did well.

Walking to school was a big responsibility, a big accomplishment to say the least. Each day I left with the group of girls from Cole Cottage. Together we walked down the sidewalk and up the hill to the old brick school building with the double front doors.

There were three floors of classrooms. My kindergarten class was located in the basement. There were windows all along the hall, looking into the room. From my vantage point at my little round table, I could see the other children of the school walk by as they hurried to get to class before the bell rang.

I enjoyed school. It wasn't much different from what I did every day. I played and learned with the other children; some of my classmates were girls that lived with me at the cottage. We were all friends and enjoyed being in the same class.

As I headed off to school one spring morning, my adventuresome spirit took me off the beaten path. I normally walked past the old neighborhoods with their rows of houses, and each day my trek led me to the front of the school with its big double doors. Down into the basement I would go and take my seat with the other children at my table.

But today was different; today, something caught my attention. I was drawn, not to the school but to someplace very magical.

Some of the old streets of Akron were paved with bricks. The old neighborhoods near the school were so beautiful with their large two-story houses, tree-lined streets, and narrow driveways. In the back of each house was a small one-car garage. Heavy rains the night before pooled on the red bricks, covering the street like a lake of water reflecting the trees that lined both sides. It was beautiful and mesmerizing. I knew I should have gone with the other children as they continued their walk, but I didn't. I spent hours wandering up and down the sidewalks, my eyes taking it all in. The day was sunny, and the morning air was cool. I could see my breath.

The air had an earthy smell, like the smell that happens right after it rains. Everything seemed so green and fresh. The moss on the sidewalk was slippery, so I had to be careful to not lose my footing. Chipmunks, chasing each other, scurried across the sidewalk, stopping only a moment to look at me and then vanish out of sight up one of the tall trees.

I knew I shouldn't be there, but I didn't care. No one was around, so there was no one to question me. I wandered for hours, fully enjoying every minute of my truancy. I stood in the middle of the street with the water surrounding me, nearly covering the toes on my shoes. The reflection of the trees in the water was so beautiful. Staring at it made me dizzy.

As I waded my day away, not realizing how late it was, I heard the afternoon bell from the school ring, giving permission for all to leave. As I headed to the front of the school, the double doors opened to spill out the "good" children from their day of learning. Drawn back into the reality that I had to get home, this sudden wave of students made it easy for me. I found my way to the group I usually walked with and headed back down the hill to Cole Cottage. Thinking about how much fun I had that day, I was not about to tell anyone where I had been, and so I didn't.

Lessons Learned

Across the street from Cole Cottage was a large playground. From time to time all of us girls would go over to play. The playground equipment was much bigger than what we had in our backyard, making it more of a challenge. Having an adult around was always a good idea so someone could keep an eye on us while we played. We were allowed to play on the equipment across the street, but not unless we were accompanied by an adult. But that didn't stop me.

The street in front of Cole Cottage was usually quiet; there were seldom any cars. The dome-shaped jungle gym was placed stoically in the middle of the playground, as if to say, "I'm the best." It was the biggest and tallest of all the equipment. Many times, I had tried to climb to the top of it, wanting all the other children to see how brave I was. Each time I was defeated by my inability to conquer my fear of heights. Try as I might, each time I had to humble myself and watch in envy as the other girls seemed to have no trouble with the task.

It was a quiet day. The girls were all outside playing in the backyard of the cottage. As I looked across the street, I decided to venture out to the "other playground" and again face my fear head on.

I approached the dome, taking in the full enormity of it. I slowly began the journey. Hand up, foot up, hand up, foot up. Taking my time, I finally maneuvered closer and closer to the top, stopping only occasionally to catch my breath. Looking up to the top, contemplating how many more steps were required to reach my goal, all while trying not to look down. Inch by inch, my progress was becoming clearer. "I can make it, just a little further. I'm almost there!" Finally making it to the top of the jungle gym, I couldn't help but yell, "Hey, look, I did it!" I wanted everyone to see what an amazing thing I had just done. The only problem was no one was watching because no one knew I was there.

Realizing no one was coming to help, my thought process began to change. Terror gripped my six-year-old heart. I thought, *Now how am I going to get down?* I was so busy getting to the top that the thought of getting down never crossed my mind. I couldn't just swing my leg around like I used to do on Grandpa's truck. This was much higher.

Praying, "God, if you can hear me...," I sat frozen for quite a while as I contemplated what to do next. I knew I would eventually get down...but how? I mustered up the courage to begin maneuvering my way back the way I came. I slowly, carefully, step by step, made my way back to the ground. How could I have done all of this and no one saw me?

I never did climb that jungle gym again. Maybe God wanted me to learn a lesson on being humble. Maybe He wanted me to learn how to trust Him to conquer my fears. What I do know is He got me out of that predicament, but to this day, I'm still afraid of heights.

*****

The street that Cole Cottage was on was, for the most part, a private street. Only the cars of the house moms and workers occasionally made their way in and out of our little neighborhood. So seeing a strange car parked at the top of the hill was quite unusual.

It had been sitting there for several days. It was parked at an angle and the windows were down. My roommates and I were curious and decided to get a closer look. A picnic table was sitting on the pavement at the front of the car, and behind that was grass and trees.

We had heard about drive-in movies but had never been to one. What harm could be done if we just pretend for a while. Two girls got into the front seat. I, on the other hand, was the entertainment. Standing on the table, I began to put on a show, dancing and singing and laughing at the girls while they were laughing at me. I watched from where I was standing as the girl that was seated in the driver's seat suddenly reached over and grabbed the gear shift lever and pulled it down.

The car, now out of gear, began to roll. The girls looked at me, their eyes and mouths wide open. I stood frozen as the car with the girls rolled backward partway down the hill and into a utility pole. Everything happened like it was in slow motion. My feet felt as if they were stuck to the table and I couldn't move. Just then the house-mother came running out of the door, yelling and waving her hands. Finally snapping out of it, I jumped off the table and ran for the car. As both of us ran, we made it to the stopped car at about the same time. Dodie and Robin were now crying, and all I could think of was, *We are in so much trouble. We didn't know it was dangerous. We were only playing!*

The two black and white cars with the red lights on top left an impression on me as all of us girls watched from inside the safety of the house. The car had been abandoned; eventually they towed it away. I guess we all learned a lesson that day about never getting into strange cars. I, of course, didn't do anything wrong because I never got in the car. I was only on the table. At least that was the reasoning I told myself at the time.

My good friends, Dodie and Robin, were the girls that were in the car when it rolled down the hill. The three of us enjoyed playing…when we weren't getting into trouble. We had spent a lot of time as roommates at Cole Cottage, and we loved each other like we were sisters.

*****

The bedrooms in the house allowed three girls to a room. My bed was located in the middle of the small room. Dodie's bed was on one side and Robin's was on the other. Each night we would go through our nightly routine and crawl into our own little beds. I always thought of the story of *The Three Little Bears* and thought it was fun to imagine myself as Momma Bear. I knew someday I wanted to be a mommy, even though I wasn't sure how a mommy was supposed to be.

Dodie and Robin were now asleep, but I was still wide awake. It seemed I was always the last to fall asleep. Most times, I was too busy thinking about whatever that day had brought. Except for an occasional trip to the bathroom, the nights were usually quiet, and my thoughts would again take me to my unanswered questions. As the girls slept, I sat at the head of my bed and looked out the big window down to the city lights below. I was getting older and I was beginning to think more about my situation at Cole Cottage.

I remembered living at my grandmother's house. I remembered living at my aunt's house. I often reflected on the fun I used to have in Cambridge. I was still confused and questioning my circumstances, so I would often pray. I was told by my Sunday school teacher that God always hears our prayers. Sleepily, I snuggled down under the covers and closed my eyes. In the darkness of my room I prayed. In the stillness of the night, in the quiet of Cole Cottage, when I was only six years old, God *did* hear my prayers.

Dearly Departed

Taking six little girls to church each week was a true act of love and patience on the housemother's part. Proper attire was always encouraged—white gloves, pretty hats, and either white or black patent shoes, depending on the season, of course. Teaching small children is so important. I had never attended church before the children's home, and I am forever grateful for the values they had instilled in me when I was a resident.

I believe it was a Baptist church, and I enjoyed going, partially because we could dress up in our pretty dresses. I was so proud to earn my first Bible in Mrs. Ruby Betts' class. It was awarded to me for memory work. It was a Living New Testament. The cover of the Bible had a picture of Jesus walking with two little children, a boy and a girl. I always pretended that the girl was me. On the inside cover it said, "Presented to Sandra Cole By: Ruby Betts, awarded for memory work on April 28, 1972." The verse was John 3:16, "For God so loved the world, that He gave His only begotten Son, that whoever believes in Him shall not perish, but have eternal life" (NASB). I was so thrilled. I had never earned anything before, and it felt great!

Each week we attended class, and each week I learned something new. God was beginning to work on my heart. I was now seven and well aware of my desire to disobey. Strong-willed and confused, I was later told that was how I coped with all the changes I had gone through. But now I was learning something other than my selfish ways. I was beginning to learn about Jesus, and I loved hearing the stories that were read to us from the Bible.

*****

I wasn't sure I wanted to go with our house mother to the funeral home. She had received news of the death of a loved one earlier that week. I was old enough to know that people die. After all, that was what I was told happened to my mother. We had talked about death briefly in Sunday school. It was all so new to me. I believe it was a relative that passed, but I'm not sure.

It was a rainy night and it was cold outside. All of us girls dressed appropriately in our little winter coats with the fake fur for a collar. Just because we were in the children's home didn't mean we couldn't dress in style. We all piled into the car and headed to the funeral home. None of us knew anything of what we were about to see.

The lights were low, and we were told to stay close, not wander off, and not talk. I don't think any of us wanted to anyway. As we entered the large room, the smell of flowers filled the air. Someone was crying softly at the front. A long line had formed and was moving slowly. As we (our housemother and us six little girls) took a place at the end of the line, I could tell where the smell of flowers was coming from. Large metal stands with bright-colored roses and carnations stood at the front of the room. Beside the flowers was a long shiny brown box. I could see that half of the box was open. A small table with framed pictures was next to it. People dressed in black were picking up the framed photos and smiling they seemed to reminisce about what they saw.

The air in the room felt heavy, and I was getting warm. We still had on our coats; we were told to leave them on because we weren't going to stay for long. Someone approached our housemother; they hugged. As I glanced up at the woman, I could see that she had been crying quite a lot. I cried like that once when I fell and skinned my knee. The look she had was one of great sadness.

The line began to move, and my heart began to race. I looked around at the people in the room. Some of them were sitting on red cushioned chairs that were lined up, side by side, in rows. As my eyes searched the room, I caught the glance of an elderly woman. She had very white hair and it was piled high on top of her head. The lady smiled at me. Not knowing what to do, I grabbed the hand of our housemother and hid behind her as she stood talking to yet another person who was crying. I closed my eyes tight, being certain that doing so would make me instantly invisible. After a moment, I got the courage to peek out from behind my housemother. The lady who had smiled at me had turned and was talking to someone else. My superpower had, yet again, saved me.

Oh, when were we going to leave this sad, sad place? The closer we got to the front of the line, the easier it was to see what was in the brown box. "It's okay, touch her!" she encouraged me. My house-mother's hand was lovingly placed on the dearly departed. I could sense the emotion and the love she felt as she touched the hand that lay still on the lifeless body. Oh no, no, no! That was the last thing I was going to do. It may be okay for you to touch but not for me!

Death… This is what it looks like. How scary. Is this what happened to my mother? So many questions filled my mind. I kept my hands plunged deep into my coat pockets and I didn't take them out until I got back to the house and had to change into my pajamas.

Dodi and Robin began chasing each other. Giggling and squealing, they took turns tagging the other, saying, "You're it!" Jumping into bed, out of breath from playing, they seemed to be so caught up in the fun they were having that they forgot what they had just witnessed.

As I pulled my covers up to my chin, I tried to put the events of that night to the back of my mind, but the questions I had puzzled me. Not really knowing the answers to any of them, I began to drift slowly to sleep. In the quiet of the house, I listened to the ticktock of the cat clock. God, are you there?

God, If You're Listening

Of all my assigned social workers, she was my favorite. I loved her. She was young and pretty. Social workers, quite often, were women. They were assigned children to manage under their care. These professionals kept the best interest of the children in mind. They worked hard to protect them in all situations and made sure that the children's needs were met. Placing children in foster homes was a top priority, and my case was no exception.

My social worker checked on me from time to time. We would go into my room at Cole Cottage. I would sit on my little bed, and she would sit on the other bed across from me. We would talk about all kinds of things. I told her of my love for animals and that I wanted to live on a farm, so if she could find me a home on a farm, I would be grateful. She wanted to know if I was happy and if school was going well. She always dressed nice and she smelled good too.

In her purse were at least half a dozen lipsticks. As she talked to me, she would keep my attention by letting me play with her makeup. She was so patient as she sat on my bed and allowed me to apply on her lips every color of lipstick that she had in her little makeup bag. Coat after coat, I would apply, and she would let me. I knew she sincerely cared for me. She was soft-spoken and was a true example of patience and kindness.

*****

Around the corner from Cole Cottage were other houses. Each day we would pass them as we walked to school. I always wondered what the houses were for. I had always seen older kids coming in and out but never really understood the significance. We never went into the buildings. There was no need to…until one afternoon.

All of us girls from Cole Cottage went as a group. We were on a tour. Most times when people want to adopt, they want a younger child, more than likely an infant. The kids we saw in these houses were the older children, teenagers that had been in the system for many years and had not found a forever home. Just like our house, the homes were divided up into the girls' house and the boys' house.

The homes were very nice. They had nicely furnished bedrooms and a common area where the kids would hang out. I remember the windows—each room had a window that would look out into the large hallway. As we walked down the hall, a girl looked out of her window. I felt her eyes follow me as our little group made its way toward the door. I wondered about her and how long she had been here. Did she like it? She was older than me, but not by much. Will she ever have a forever home or a farm with lots of animals? Questions again bounced around in my head as we continued the tour. "God, if you're listening, please don't let me end up here…please."

*****

Life wasn't bad when I lived at the children's home. They took very good care of us girls. Kind people were always doing things for us, making us laugh, bringing us toys or candy. There were always people coming and going.

During the day, people would visit. We didn't pay much attention; we were too busy playing. I now understand. Families looking to adopt or foster a child would want to see the children so they could see which child would be a suitable match. Careful planning to match the child up with the right family was of highest importance. Usually, the child was given the opportunity to visit a potential home before a final decision was made. I was soon told that I would be visiting a family. This home I was to visit could potentially be the one for me.

My behavior had greatly improved during the time I was placed in Cole Cottage. After being there for several years, a foster home was identified for me. I was one of the lucky ones. I was older, and like I had said before, most people want infants instead of seven-year-olds. It wasn't a family with a farm, but they had a dog! They say that I immediately went and packed my bags after learning that I would be leaving. It wasn't long before I moved out of Cole Cottage and into my new home. It was the day after Father's Day, June 1972.

My social worker pulled up and parked on the street next to Cole Cottage. I had packed my bag, which contained all that I owned, and I quickly gave it to her to place in the trunk of her car.

I looked back at the cottage, to the home where I had lived for nearly two years. All of the girls had come outside and had lined up along the fence by the front gate to watch me go. I looked at each one as I said goodbye before I got into the car. Dodie and Robin were sad to see me leave. I waved out the car window as we drove away from the house. Some of the girls were smiling and waving while others just watched. I was happy for myself but couldn't help but wonder if the day would come for them to find a family that wanted them.

It was about a half-hour drive to get to my new home. As we exited the highway, we continued for about a block and then turned down a street that was lined with houses. I was anxious to get there. I had the opportunity to visit it more than once over a period of several months, but today was different. Today I knew I would stay. The house was located at the very end of the neighborhood. It was big with a nice yard and lots of trees. The neighbor's house had a long driveway that connected to the drive we were approaching. Beautiful yellow and orange marigold flowers lined the way. After we came to a stop, my social worker announced, "We're here." I quickly opened the car door and got out as she lifted my bag from the trunk.

It was a warm Monday afternoon. As a door from inside the garage opened, my new family came out to greet us: Dad, Mom, and three brothers—Brian, Blaine, and Bruce.

I was happy to see them. I had enjoyed our visits prior to the Pecks becoming my foster family, but what caught my attention was the little dog my new dad was carrying in his arms. Her name was Duchess; she was a dachshund. I finally had a dog! As Dad set her down, she came running to greet me. She sniffed me for only a moment and then ran into the yard to explore. I had been matched with a complete family. The closest I had to brothers in the past were my two cousins. Now I had not just two but three brothers. What an overwhelming and happy day it was.

Many years later when I was grown, my parents told me of how they had prayed that the Lord would give them the right little girl, the one that He wanted them to have. They weren't looking for an infant—they had three older sons and were way past that stage in their lives. They wanted a little girl that was adventuresome and enjoyed the outdoors as much as they did. And that's just what He gave them.

Me with my three brothers, Bruce, Blaine, and Brian

My Way!

I continued with some counseling after I moved in with the Pecks. I remember going to several classes over a short period of time. I don't recall the details of where I was, but I do remember the room. The room was small and colorful with several tables and rows of toys that were placed on shelves against the walls. A woman, probably a case worker, sat and talked with me during those times. On one of the walls in the classroom was a large mirror that I was very curious about. I later discovered that there was a secret room behind that mirror. This room was where observers could monitor the children's behavior during their sessions.

I also found where they hid the snacks, and I remember eating as many graham crackers as I could before someone stopped me. When I was older, I learned that this program was specifically designed to monitor foster and adopted children to be sure they were adjusting to their new home. I had a lot of changes very quickly when I moved in with the Pecks. These sessions were to be sure I was managing all of those changes well.

The Pecks did a lot to make my transition as easy as they could. They built an addition onto the house to accommodate their growing family. Brian, my oldest brother, gave up his bedroom for me while my other two brothers shared a bedroom.

I had my own room down the hall to the right. Three windows on the far wall looked out onto a big maple tree. Yellow daffodils were blooming under it. The shade from the tree blocked the direct sunlight from streaming in and left a warm glow to the room. One wall was decorated in colored, striped wallpaper. There was a big bed that had a headboard that matched the nightstand. On the nightstand was a delicate little lamp with a pretty, white shade.

The closet was also big, not like the one I had at the children's home. A large dresser with a mirror attached stood opposite the bed. It wasn't purple like my previous room at my aunt's house, and it was a lot bigger than my room at my grandmother's house. Unlike the children's home, I didn't have to share it with two other girls!

To help me adjust to all of the changes, my foster parents went to Cole Cottage where I used to live. Picking up all six little girls, they took us out for a treat of ice cream at an outdoor ice cream shop called Stricklands. It was across from the Akron Municipal Airport. It first opened in 1936, and although it was a local favorite in the area for many years, this was a new experience for me. It was a rare treat for all of the girls to go out for ice cream. We usually only got ice cream once a week when we all sat together to watch *The Wonderful World of Disney* on TV.

Seven little girls, all wanting ice cream, all crowding around my foster dad saying, "Daddy, Daddy, Daddy." As he recalled this story later in life, he always laughed about the looks he got from the other customers. Here he was with seven girls, all aged six or seven years old, representing a broad cross-section of diversity and calling him daddy. He just simply smiled back to all of the confused onlookers. I was happy to see the girls. Some of them I had lived with for the two years I had been at the children's home. Transitioning into my new family was yet another big change in my life, and Mom and Dad knew I needed to do it slowly. Saying goodbye over time to my friends would not be easy, but I was ready to be a part of a real family. So until I said goodbye for good, I enjoyed my visits with my friends.

My two roommates from Cole Cottage, Dodie and Robin, often came to my house to spend the day. All three of us would enjoy playing in my room. I didn't always want to share my newfound toys or my new family with the girls. I remembered how Dodie had gotten a Big Wheel riding toy one Christmas at Cole Cottage. Remembering that Christmas, I thought to myself, *These are my toys now.* Jealousy can be an ugly thing in a seven-year-old girl. It had a way of taking over, and before long I would get angry. I had a lot to learn about sharing and not being selfish, and now I finally had new parents to teach me.

*****

I was seven years old when I went to live with the Pecks. Another new place to live, new people I didn't know, new schools, new friends, new rules, and a new mom. When it came to my new mom, I had finally met my match.

I couldn't get away with fooling my new mom like I could my aunt. Mom would set the kitchen timer that was located on the stove. I had five minutes to finish my dinner and then it was taken away from me. There would be no food until breakfast the next day. "Who is in control here? I'm not going to eat, and you can't make me!"

If I'd only known the battle that would play out! My will was strong, but Mom's was stronger. She didn't bat an eye when I refused to do things her way. After I refused to eat, she took my plate and said, "Okay, go play." Ha! That was easy. I had won...or at least so I thought.

Later that evening, I, of course, was hungry. Sticking to her rule, she wouldn't give in. It didn't take long for me to learn that I had to eat at dinnertime or be faced with going to bed hungry.

That would not be the end of my "teaching moments" with my mom. After a routine checkup at the dental office, my new mom was told that I had six cavities and they needed to be filled. I certainly did not brush my teeth as well as I ought when I was at the children's home, and trips down Clark Street to the local five-and-dime to buy candy with the girls had taken its toll on me.

Trusting the children's home would take care of my dental situation, my mom arranged for a social worker to pick me up and take me to the dental clinic that was located in the main building.

As we drove down the highway, I remember seeing a big clock tower that I affectionately called Big Ben. Akron used to be the rubber capital of the world. Tires were made by Goodyear in the large factories located close to the children's home. Big Ben was a part of one of the buildings where the tires were made. As we drove to my appointment, I could see the large red-bricked smokestacks. Gray smoke was rising upward out of the tops of the big stacks that had, over time, gathered soot. As soon as I saw Big Ben, I knew we were almost there.

The anxiety I had knowing what was about to come was almost too much. I was terrified of the dentist and associated him with the pain from past experiences. We pulled up to the stately old building, and I slowly got out of the car. The good memories of being in the medical clinic and the kind nurses were nowhere near what I was about to experience as I proceeded to the "other" clinic.

The social worker escorted me down a long hallway. I stalled as long as I could by tilting my head back so I could look up at the tall ceiling. Running my hand along the chair rail, I continued to look up as I tried to prolong the inevitable, but this only made me dizzy. Almost tripping myself, I looked back down and focused my eyes again on the linoleum floor.

Along the hall were several doors. I never saw anyone go in or out of those doors. I had wondered what was behind them. Around the corner, halfway down the hall, was the dental office. Opening the door to the office terrified me. There was a unique smell, the one that only comes from a dental office, part antiseptic and part clove oil. It happened to be quiet that day, unlike the usual sounds of drilling and grinding. I walked in and took a seat.

The reception room was small with metal chairs lining the walls. The only windows were the ones in the operatories. They had children's books scattered on a few small tables. I always enjoyed looking at the *Highlights* magazine, but who goes to the dentist to read? The only way of escape was out the way I came in.

It was my turn. I climbed into the chair. I had to think quickly. I needed a plan. I just won't open my mouth! Try as they did, I wasn't going to cooperate.

My mom was furious when the social worker brought me back home with six cavities that still needed to be filled. I had no idea what I had gotten myself in for. On my next appointment, she went with me!

This time I opened my mouth, but I fought long and hard. As the dentist tried to do his job, I smacked the drill out of his hand and into the hand of the assistant. She wrapped her finger up in gauze. Her injury didn't require any stitches, but she wasn't happy with me. The doctor strapped the nitrous mask on me. I calmed down enough to allow them to do their job. Eventually all the cavities were filled, and Mom was happy.

As our family sat at the dinner table that night discussing my dental woes, Blaine—now on his second helping of food and me still on my first—said, "Tonight, before bed, I want to see how you brush your teeth." How exciting could that be? I know he was trying to help so I wouldn't get any more cavities, so reluctantly, I agreed.

Nine o'clock rolled around, and just like Blaine had promised, he followed me into the bathroom like he was Sherlock Holmes. "Go ahead, brush your teeth." Taking my toothbrush out of the drawer, I proceeded to place the toothpaste on my brush. "That's your problem!" he said, "You are using hardly any toothpaste!" Then taking my toothbrush in his hand, he proceeded to show me how he did it. Sure enough, the amount I was using was nowhere near what it should be. Proud of himself for figuring out my problem, he showed me the right way. Once he was sure I had it, his work was finished, and he exited the room.

As I think back now, it was a small thing for Blaine to do for me. I never had a brother come alongside of me before and help. This was all so new. This is what a family does for each other. I am thankful for a big brother that loved me enough to care.

Christmas Dress

Mom and me on the white sofa my first Christmas with the Pecks

It was my first Christmas in my new home. The smell of food I had never tasted before filled the house. Beautiful decorations seemed to be around every corner. Vanilla- and cinnamon-scented candles were placed throughout the house, ready to light when the time was right.

There was a decoration that especially caught my eye—a manger scene. It was simple, made of wood with plaster figurines. Mom knew I liked it, so she asked me if I would like to set up the characters. I paid special attention to give baby Jesus the position of importance that He deserved. In the living room was the Christmas tree; it was covered in colored lights and thin strips of silver icicles that glistened each time the lights would twinkle. We had to keep an eye on Duchess, since she liked to eat the icicles when we weren't looking. Eating too many of them made her sick, as we learned when we found the undigested decorations in piles around the house.

Dodie and Robin came for a visit that Christmas. They still had not found their forever homes. I was happy to see them. We loved cookies, and we enjoyed working together as we helped bake them. While we waited for the cookies to cool, we helped Mom decorate the Christmas tree. The cookies we made were one of Grandma Kmetz's recipes. Grandma Kmetz was Mom's mom. I helped Mom make the dough the day before and let it sit in the refrigerator overnight. The next day Blaine helped as we all rolled out the dough and used cookie cutters to make Christmas shapes. Once the cookies were baked and cooled, we were able to decorate them with icing and colored sprinkles. They were so good; it was hard not to eat them as soon as they were decorated.

Robin, Dodie, and me decorating the tree my first Christmas with the Pecks

Dodie, Robin, Mom, me, and Blaine (L–R) making Christmas cookies my first Christmas with the Pecks

The living room was more formal than the other rooms, which meant we only used it for special occasions. I had never lived in a house so fancy before. Under the Christmas tree was a package, and I was told I could open it early before we left for the Christmas Eve service at church. I don't think I have ever been so excited in all my life to open a present. To be honest, I never really got many presents before.

I was told not to touch it. Saying that to a seven-year-old is like saying, "I dare you to touch it!" It wasn't a heavy package. It was actually quite light for its size. My brothers were watching TV; Dad was getting ready. I knew Mom wouldn't be around because she still had things to do in the kitchen. I was told to go and take the pink foam rollers out of my hair that had been in for most of the day.

As much as I wanted to obey, the temptation was just too great. The room was now getting dark, the sun was setting, and the only lights were the colored ones that lit up the tree. As I picked up the package, I saw that a corner of the wrapping paper was not adhered tightly by the tape Mom had used. It didn't take much to pull the paper to the side. Peeking, I could tell it was a white box, the kind clothes come in when you buy them new. Folding down the corner, I was able to stick my right finger in just enough to feel what was inside. It was soft but I couldn't see. The small clue I had felt left my mind wondering, *What could it be?* Placing the box carefully back under the tree, I slipped down the hall to my room and closed the door.

All the preparations for the evening were finished. The snow was glistening as the sun finally set over the trees in the backyard. It was time. I ran into the living room, grabbed the present from under the tree, and tore it open. I could hardly contain myself as I took the lid off and moved the white paper back to reveal a beautiful long colorful dress. I pulled it out of the box and held it up, tucking it under my chin so it wouldn't fall. I could feel a big smile come over my face. Mom had made matching dresses for our first Christmas together. Of all the dresses I had ever owned, this was by far the most beautiful. I quickly ran to put it on.

The top part of the dress was blue, and the bottom half was multicolored. It had a blue velvet ribbon that tied around my waist. Mom went to her room to change and soon came out with her matching dress. Hers was just as beautiful. The collar was embellished with pearls that she had sewn into the neckline.

*Me proudly holding the dress Mom had made
for me on our first Christmas together*

Mom's hair was shoulder length, which she wore slightly curled. My hair, now out of the pink curlers, still needed to be brushed. As we styled my hair, we looked into the mirror and smiled; neither one spoke. Looking quite nice, we posed for pictures on the white sofa in the fancy living room. It was going to be a great Christmas.

*****

I had never been to a Christmas Eve service. The church was decorated much the same way home was—beautiful lights, the smell of candles burning, and music filling the air. I always thought Christmas was about presents and Santa. I was learning that it was so much more! God, in His wisdom, had taken me out of an unstable situation and placed me in the family that was going to be best suited for me. We may not understand at times why He allows things to happen the way they do. Things were beginning to fall into place. God was opening my eyes, and I was learning.

I liked where I was, I liked my family, I liked my school, and I liked my new church. I guess I even liked my brothers, even if they would tease me. I especially liked my dog. I had made a new friend at church—Lori. Her last name was Clark. My last name was Cole. So we affectionately gave each other nicknames. She was Clark Bar and I was Coleslaw. We were both seven and thought we were so clever. Whoever got to church first would wait by the long window by the front door until the other one arrived. Lori and I did everything together; we even went to the same school. We promised each other that when we grew up, we would be roommates and share an apartment. She was my best friend.

Although I was adjusting nicely to my new world, I wondered, *Would this be the final place or would someone from the children's home come back to get me and take me to yet another home?* I had so many memories and questions. "What had happened to my grandmother?" I couldn't remember the last time I saw her. Once a child is placed in foster care, the natural family normally is no longer a part of that child's life. Hoping the foster or adoptive family would be a good match, SCCS didn't allow visits from natural family members. Records were kept private; even my aunt and uncle had no idea where I had been placed. Happy where I was, I prayed, "God, I know you can hear me. I hope they don't come back for me. This time I want to stay!"

The girls I lived with for two years while I was a resident at Cole Cottage. This picture was taken in the living room of the cottage on one of our visits back to the house after I was placed with the Pecks.

Into the Woods

I loved my bike. What a great Christmas present it had been. Learning to ride was my next challenge. Our street was the perfect place. Not much traffic, only the occasional neighbor coming home from work. I stayed right out front where the road had a bend that curved back out onto the main road. I was so proud of myself when I finally got the hang of riding it. I spent all of my spare time riding up and down those two streets. I was now eight years old and fully enjoying my accomplishment.

It was yellow with a basket in front, tall handlebars with long flowing plastic fringe that would blow in the wind when I would pedal really fast. On the back of the seat hung a small metal license plate that read, "Sandy." Bruce had shown me how to attach a couple of playing cards to the spokes of the wheel so that they would hit the spokes and make a noise as I pedaled. The banana seat wasn't that comfortable, but I stood most of the time.

My outfit was an interesting one—T-shirt and shorts, because the summer was hot, and white go-go boots that I had also gotten for Christmas. My long, light brown hair hung down my back and occasionally stuck to my face when I got too sweaty.

The woods behind my new home had many trees and trails to ride on. Heading through the side yard, I cut across the back of the house. The trail started behind the neighbor's property and led through the woods to a field that the kids around the block used for baseball. On the other side of the field was an opening in the trees. I would ride my bike with some of the girls that lived by me. We spent many hours exploring. My brothers used the trails with their minibikes, so it was well worn and easy to follow. Long rides took me to a dirt road. I think the farmer who owned the property drove his tractor down that road when he worked out in his fields. Following the dirt road as far as I could, I was able to see the farm located across the street from my grade school. Mr. Towner, who would eventually become one of my teachers in middle school, lived there. He always kept an eye on his property, and if he thought us kids were spooking his horses, he would come out of his house in his blue jean overalls and shoo us away. He was a kind man, but he meant business if you spooked his horses.

Streams and small ponds were here and there throughout the woods. In the winter I would ice skate on the larger ones. My favorite was a pond that was lined with cattails. I named it Cattail Pond. Muskrats would build their dens on the ice. I had to be careful to pay attention while I was skating so I didn't run into one of them. It was quiet there. I had spent many hours skating, pretending that I was a professional skater like the girls in the Ice Capades.

I wanted to bring a friend, so I asked Shannon, my neighbor, if she wanted to come with me. We had spent a lot of time together riding bikes as we played around the neighborhood. I had stayed overnight at her house on several different occasions. Friday nights were fun because we would ride our bikes to the gas station that was located over the hill by our neighborhood. Shannon and I would buy all of the Atomic Fireballs and Tootsie Rolls they had in their small country store. We liked going to her house because her mom let us stay up late watching scary movies. Shannon and I would gather all the pillows and blankets we could and plop ourselves right in front of the TV. We spent many nights lying on the floor in her living room watching *Big Chuck and Lil' John*. They were late-night TV horror hosts back in the late '70s and early '80s. One night we watched a movie that had Medusa in it. Medusa was a monster that had the face of an ugly woman with snakes instead of hair. Anyone who looked into her eyes was immediately turned to stone. It was only a myth, but Shannon didn't care. Jumping on top of me, she covered my eyes with the closest blanket while yelling, "Don't look! You'll turn to stone!" Laughing, we knew it wasn't true, but we liked to scare each other when we could.

Shannon and I learned to skate together. We first learned to roller skate down in my basement. It was cooler there in the summer, so we would spend time skating in circles trying to catch each other. Now during the winter months between the rain and the snow, the end of my driveway would often flood and freeze leaving a patch of ice that was big enough for us to ice skate on. All the kids in the neighborhood would gather on those rare occasions and skate until it got dark. That was a good starting place for me, but I soon found out that the ponds in the woods behind my house were bigger and more fun.

It had been very cold and snowy for about a week, and knowing from experience, I figured the water was probably quite frozen. I was hopeful that my favorite spot, Cattail Pond, would be solid enough for skating. It was a Saturday, and the sun was out. I decided I wanted to share my special place with Shannon.

With skates in hand, we stepped out the back door of my house. I told Shannon that it was a bit of a walk, so she just needed to follow me. I looked forward to spending the morning skating. I knew that the area where the pond was located would be beautiful. The snow had settled on the branches of the trees, which made everything sparkle when the sun hit it. We needed to get to the pond today because the sun was out and, within a few days, it wouldn't be safe to skate.

As we hiked through the snow and tall plants to get to it, I had a feeling we wouldn't be there long. Tired already? We weren't even there yet! Sitting by one of the muskrat dens, we put on our skates. As Shannon struggled with her skates, I was already exploring the ice. I looked to the far end and noticed that the ice was a little too thin to support us. Just as I was turning around to let her know we needed to stay on the other side, she skirted past me, knock-kneed and a little off balance. It was too late. I reached out, hoping to grab her, but the sleeve of her coat slipped through my glove.

It was a cold walk back to my house. I felt bad for her. Always the optimist, I reminded her that at least she didn't fall in all the way. Taking off her soaked right sock, she put on her dry boots. Several layers of clothing—long johns and a pair of jeans—were soaking wet up to her knee on her right leg. She was shivering by the time we walked all the way back home. I let Shannon borrow a pair of jeans since hers were wet. It felt so good to get into some dry clothes and enjoy a cup of hot cocoa with tiny marshmallows. We decided to take a break from the snow and play inside for the rest of the afternoon.

*****

Whether it was winter or summer, the woods became my playground. I spent hours outside playing, hiking, and riding my bike. Once in a while, I would come across a snake or deer. Of course, I ran from the snakes but stood as still as I could to watch the deer. I only went home when I knew it was getting late.

Because we lived so close to the woods, daddy longlegs were often seen crossing our path. Bruce liked to catch them and let them walk up his arms while he tried to scare me. Eventually, he couldn't do that anymore, not after I got the nerve to handle them myself.

One day, I got creative and went for a long walk on one of the trails. I was looking for sassafras plants. Pulling the plant up to expose the roots, I loved to deeply breathe in the aroma. The root of the plant smelled so good, like I was smelling root beer. After a while, I felt I had collected enough and headed home to clean the roots and boil them in water to make sassafras tea. Convincing myself that it tasted good, I offered a sip to anyone who was brave enough to try it. Eventually, I had to admit that it smelled better than it tasted. I took one last sniff and threw the rest out.

*****

Mom liked it when I gave her special things, like most moms do, whether it was a picture I made at school, which she would proudly display on the refrigerator, or a craft, or even beautiful yellow dandelions. One summer afternoon, I rode my bike to the end of the road where the drainpipe that ran under the highway emptied into the ditch that ran through our neighborhood. I called it my "wishing well." The small lot that was located next to it was usually covered in dandelions around midsummer. After I was finished plopping my small pebbles in the wishing well while making my wishes, I gathered a handful of dandelions to take to Mom.

I was so proud when I presented her my bouquet. There were at least a dozen of them, and I knew the yellow color of the flower was her favorite. Dandelions happen to be full of pollen. There's a saying that you could tell if someone likes butter by rubbing the bloom from the dandelion under their chin. If the pollen came off and left its yellow dust, then they liked butter.

What a wonderful gift for a young girl to bring her mom—or at least I thought it was. Holding the fresh picked surprise in one hand, I maneuvered my bike with the other. I didn't have to pedal much; the wishing well and field of dandelions were on a hill, so I coasted down to the driveway and quickly dropped my bike in the yard. I entered the house through the door in the open garage just in time to see Mom about to leave the kitchen. As I caught Mom's eye, I smiled big as I proudly handed her the flowers. Mom hesitated for a moment and then took the dandelions. She thanked me and proceeded to take a vase out of the kitchen cabinet and fill it with water. As she placed the vase and flowers on the windowsill, she told me how nice it was for me to pick her flowers. All day long those dandelions sat on the kitchen windowsill. Not until I was older did I realize she had terrible allergies, and pollen, especially from dandelions, was one of them.

As the last day of summer came to an end, I put my bike away in the metal shed behind the house. I unlatched the padlock using the combination—one click to the right, then back, one click to the left, then back, last click to the right—opens every time! Pushing the kickstand down with my right foot, I squeezed my bike in between the lawn mower and my brother Bruce's twelve-speed. The big trees in the backyard gave relief from the heat. In another month the leaves would change color and begin to fall. School was getting ready to start, but I didn't want summer to end. I was about to start fifth grade.

Ms. Lolly

Greenwood Elementary School—I had already been attending Greenwood; this would be my third year since leaving Cole Cottage. Ms. Lolly was my teacher. She had long blond hair and was always smiling. Even her name was happy. She smelled nice too. Her perfume reminded me of the flowers from the meadow behind my grandmother's house. Whenever I got into trouble, she always knew how to handle the situation in a way that made me sad that I had disappointed her.

The best part about school—recess! A big playground out back, and beyond the playground were little league baseball fields where I would play girls' softball in a few years. I loved being outside. I had lots of friends. Of course, Lori was my best friend. At recess we would pretend we were cheerleaders. We stayed away from the swings. Everyone knows the best way to swing is to go as high as you possibly can, but doing that only got us into trouble. As soon as we got near the height we wanted, the playground safety patrol would yell at us to stop going so high! These kids were the privileged, chosen fifth graders who already had too much power—at least that's what I always thought. Things were going well until about the second week into the new school year.

Morning class had started. I was sitting at my desk when a man, whom I had seen before in the office, walked into the room. As he spoke with Ms. Lolly, she glanced my way. She called my name and asked me to gather my school supplies and meet her up front. Embarrassed by the unexpected attention, I did as I was told. I had been in Ms. Lolly's class because I was behind in my studies since leaving the children's home. Working on my math and reading over the summer, I had caught up. I had done so well that they were moving me to a more challenging curriculum.

No, that can't be! I don't want to leave! I love this class. My mind was racing; if they could only hear the conflict that was playing out in my head. *Where would I go? I have made new friends here!* As I left the class, I was escorted to a class across the hall and two doors down. It was a nice room, lots of windows that looked out at the trees, unlike Ms. Lolly's room that looked out onto the playground. Before I entered my new class, I glanced over my shoulder to see Ms. Lolly looking back at me. Seeing the tears in my eyes, she left the doorway of her classroom, walked over, and gave me a hug. "It will be okay," she said. "Lori is in your new class." Ms. Lolly knew she was my best friend, and she hoped this would make my transition a little easier on me. As I returned her hug, I didn't say a word. I didn't want any of the new kids to know I was crying, so I swallowed hard and wiped my face.

Mr. Harold was his name. He was nothing like my beloved Ms. Lolly. He was short, had brown curly hair, a mustache, and seemed to always wear the same suit. I don't recall him smiling much. As I sat in my seat, he did what I was hoping he wouldn't. He announced to his already-established class that I was the new student. Everyone there knew I was the new kid. I had seen these kids before but didn't really know them. The only friend I had in the whole room was Lori. Announcing my name only made me feel more uncomfortable. I felt like I was under a stage spotlight—like when my aunt opened the refrigerator door the night I was sneaking buttermilk. Only this time all eyes were on me.

I sat down at my new desk and put my supplies away. I could still smell Ms. Lolly's perfume as it lingered from the hug she had given me. My new classmates soon got back to their work and I was no longer the center of attention. It will be okay, and I will be okay. I have to be; I have no choice. I glanced at Lori; she was seated behind me a few rows. She smiled and waved; I waved back. Thankful she was there, I knew we would be spending time together at recess, which helped me to feel better.

*****

Fifth grade was when I was introduced to the possibility of playing an instrument. I enjoyed music class and was excited when the music teacher gave each student a recorder and announced how we would all learn to play and someday we could play a song together. The recorder, normally made from plastic, came with its own carrying bag. They were brown and were held similarly to a clarinet. Using both hands, I could cover the necessary holes with my fingers and the hole in back with my left thumb. Blowing on the mouthpiece, I could make it sound like a whistle or an organ pipe, depending on how hard I blew.

Mr. Harold was given instructions by the music teacher so that each day during class, he would teach us a brief lesson that we were expected to learn by practicing at home. The following day we would all play the song together, hoping this would spark the children's interest to choose an instrument of their own. This was the first step toward introducing us to the middle school band program. I had an idea of what instrument I eventually wanted to play, so Mom began the process through SCCS to see if I could get a clarinet. I chose the clarinet because it reminded me of the recorder. I didn't have a lot of confidence, and I thought it might be easier to learn.

Mr. Harold's class was more of a challenge for me academically, and I had to work hard to keep up. I wasn't a good student to begin with. Starting off at my new school when I entered second grade, I had a lot of catching up to do. Whenever I had a question, Mr. Harold would stand over my desk to see what it was I needed. As he leaned closer to see my paper, I couldn't help but notice the hair growing from inside his ears. I already had a problem with focusing, and to tell you the truth, this didn't help.

It wasn't my favorite year of school. I occasionally got into trouble. Crazy things would make Mr. Harold mad. Simple daydreaming while blowing spit bubbles would make him furious. Most of the time he would call me out and announce my behavior to the rest of the class as if I were on trial, and again, all eyes would be on me and embarrass me. I was glad when the final bell sounded that year. No longer in fifth grade, I walked as fast as I could to get to my bus. Of all the teachers I had in grade school, Ms. Lolly was always my favorite.

Oh, Brother!

My first birthday celebrated with my forever family
(Bruce and I are pictured.)

The school bus came to a stop. This was my street. I still had to walk to the end of it to get to my house. Walking with the other kids in the neighborhood was similar to when I walked to Mason school several years before. Laughing and chasing each other, we would pop tar bubbles that had formed on the road from the hot afternoon sun. We were excited; summer was finally here.

Going through the side of the garage, I noticed Mom's car was gone. I always announced, "Mom, I'm home," as I opened the kitchen door. Most of the time she was there, but on the days she wasn't, I knew the handwritten note of chores taped to the kitchen cabinet was for me. One Saturday, she asked me to clean the cinders out of the fireplace. I was in a mood that day and not wanting to do my chores. As I reluctantly shoveled the ashes into the bag to be thrown away, Mom heard me mumble that I felt like Cinderella and someday a handsome prince would come and take me away from all of this! Oh, boy, she never let me forget I said that. We laugh about it now.

It was my last day of school, and I was looking forward to our family's summer vacation. Dad would be taking time off work, so the plan was to leave next week to drive to Florida. Mom was out running errands, and I was left with the note of things she needed me to get done before dinner that night. Bruce got home from school close to the same time as me. Bruce was four years older than me, the youngest of my three brothers, and he took every opportunity to tease me when Mom wasn't looking. The family room was right off the kitchen. That was where Bruce always liked to watch TV after school, after grabbing a snack. Often, his snack consisted of the left-overs Mom was planning to use for dinner that night. With his snack in his hand, he turned on the TV and plopped himself down on the couch. I knew I had some chores to do from the note that Mom had left, so I let him know that he needed to get out of my way. Not taking "No" for an answer, I grabbed the kitchen towel and began to snap it at him. Before I could get away from him, he had bounced off the couch and headed for the kitchen sink. Taking the sprayer in his hand, he turned the water on full force and proceeded to spray me and the whole kitchen with water. I quickly grabbed a cup from the sink and began to throw water at him.

He knew he had me beat because I had to stop to reload each time I ran out of water. Our full-blown water war was in progress when Bruce looked out the kitchen window and saw Mom's car stopped at the mailbox at the end of the driveway. Mom was picking up that day's mail, as she often did before driving into the garage to park the car. "Mom's home!" We looked at each other and both thought the same thing—we're in big trouble. The floor was soaked and so were we. We grabbed any towel we could and began mopping up the floor on our hands and knees. We never moved so fast! As Mom finished getting the mail, we could hear her car as it drove up to the house. Gaining another minute as she waited for the garage door to open, we finished wiping the floor with just enough time to throw the wet towels into the washing machine in the laundry room, which was just to the back of the house.

The kitchen door opened just as Bruce and I were exiting the room. Thinking it would look like we were up to something, we stayed and said hi, to which she asked how our day went while commenting on how she was glad we would be leaving for vacation soon. Bruce and I, not wanting to talk, shook our heads in agreement and then turned to each go our own way. As she placed the shopping bags she had carried in from the car on the table, she glanced around the room and said, "This floor looks so clean." Somehow, she knows! Glancing at each other, we smiled and headed off, each to our own room. Mom was now in the laundry room putting some supplies away when I heard her say, "I thought I did all the laundry."

Mom never knew how the floor got so clean and how she ended up with more laundry. For Bruce and me, it was our little secret. I think silly things like that brought Bruce and me closer together. At the time, I was reluctant to admit it, but I really was blessed to have my big brothers.

Granny

*Brian, me, and Grandma Kmetz at the beach
on vacation in Florida at the age of seven*

Planning a vacation for six people took work. Mom and Dad chose not to fly to Florida. It was too expensive, so a two-day car ride was the only way to do it. This way we could also bring Duchess. It was an exciting trip. Mom and Dad planned fun things to do along the way to break up time in the car. We didn't normally eat many donuts, but when we traveled, Mom always got some to take along with the hard-boiled eggs she prepared the day before. I never really liked eggs. Getting me to eat one for breakfast was always one of the battles my mom and I would have. I finally figured out that if I ate them with salt it was a little easier to swallow.

Grandma Kmetz lived in Ocala, Florida. We called her Granny. She was Mom's mom. I enjoyed spending time at her house. Granny's house was small—three bedrooms and a car port that had been converted into a sun porch. There was a nice backyard where Granny enjoyed growing her favorite flowers. She always talked about how bad the tomatoes were in Florida. She had lived in many other places in her lifetime, and Florida was the worst for growing tomatoes. Granny and Mom were very close. They had been through a lot and made the best of some tough times.

Beside the sun porch, at the front of the house, was a big tree. The branches were just low enough to make it great for climbing. We stayed for several weeks when we visited Granny. I made friends with the little girl that lived across the street. Her name was Karen. Karen and I spent hours playing and climbing that tree. Once, I jumped off and twisted my ankle. Frustrated by my injury, I still tried to climb that tree until I was told to come inside and rest. I didn't want to miss out on spending time playing with Karen.

Grandma Kmetz's house and the tree we loved to climb. Here I am with two of my brothers, Blaine and Brian.

I slept in Granny's sewing room. I enjoyed looking at all the patterns she had laid across the small table to the side of her machine. She was always making something. This is where my mom got her love for sewing. There was no bed in this room, so I used my sleeping bag and slept on the floor.

Granny worked hard all her life as a waitress, and she was good at it. She had a servant's heart and a love for people. She soon retired because she had battled arthritis and at times would be in a lot of pain. Even through the pain, she loved doing things for others and especially her family.

I remember one summer when she was visiting us in Ohio and decided that she would mow the grass at the front of our house. Her arthritis was bothering her, so instead of complaining about it, she decided that the vibration of the mower would be good therapy for her ailment.

Reluctantly, I agreed to let her do the job that was intended for me. Mom wasn't home and Granny was insistent. Before she was halfway done though, Mom came home. "I tried to stop her," I said. "She wouldn't listen to me."

But Mom was concerned. "Oh my, what will the neighbors think of my seventy-year-old mother out mowing our grass in her summer dress and her orthopedic shoes?" There was nothing Mom could do. Granny was determined and she knew it.

I stood there watching to be sure she was okay. Granny continued to mow until the job was completed. With each pass she took, I couldn't help but chuckle to myself as she turned the corner and waved at me with a big smile on her face. That was my granny! She seldom let things bother her. She was always thinking of ways she could lean into a problem rather than allow the problem to get her down. At a young age I saw that quality in her and admired it.

Each year, at Christmas, Granny would send a large box of Christmas cookies. There were so many different kinds, all ones she had made herself. They were very special, so we tried to make them last as long as we could. I must admit that it was hard to do. Mom kept them in the extra refrigerator in the mud room, which made it handy to grab a few while running out the door.

Before our visits to her house in Florida, Granny would bake to stock up on special treats. Her kitchen was small, so she kept some things in other areas of the house. I wasn't intending to find her hiding spot, but one time I opened the closet door in the hallway and there it was! I was probably snooping a little.

The pickle jar full of cookies was carefully tucked to one side, next to the sets of sheets. She was frugal and liked to make use of things again if she could, so a big pickle jar made a perfect container for snickerdoodles. My love for cookies got the best of me. What a perfect place for me to sneak one or two whenever I wanted, down the hall next to the sewing room, where no one could see. I only had to be on the lookout for my brothers, who would come looking for me so they could tease me—the little sister. I had my hands full! I think Granny knew I would sneak those cookies. Somehow, I don't think she minded. I loved those visits to Granny's house, and I loved spending time with her when we would vacation together.

Snuggle Inn

Holden Beach, North Carolina, vacation house.
Blaine getting ready to hit the beach.

As a family, we loved to travel, especially to the ocean. One of our favorite locations we enjoyed was Holden Beach. Holden Beach is a beautiful seaside town in Brunswick County, North Carolina. The beachfront was lined with cottages and houses. Some of the houses were permanent residences while others were rentals. Each house or cottage had a cute name that was almost always posted on the house facing the road.

During the summers, we would rent one of two houses that were owned by the same people. The houses names were Snuggle Up and Snuggle Inn. The house we rented was big enough to accommodate all of us, which usually included Granny Kmetz, Grandma and Grandpa Peck, and occasionally a friend. Eventually our family grew to include my brother Blaine's high school sweetheart, Terri, who was now his wife.

Terri and I were sent to the closest Piggly Wiggly to buy groceries for the week as everyone else unpacked. We had a long list, so we took my parents' van. We had several shopping carts full by the time we finished. We paid for the groceries and knew that we needed to get back to the house soon so the food wouldn't spoil and the ice cream wouldn't melt. Terri took one cart and I took the other. As she shuffled through her purse, it became obvious that she couldn't find the keys. We both looked in the van where we spotted the keys dangling in the ignition, doors locked and two buggies of groceries waiting to be unloaded. We didn't know whether to laugh or cry. The van was an older model, so the style of the locks had a wide knob at the top of the narrow stem. We were very resourceful, or so we thought. A discount store was close by in the same strip mall as the grocery store, so we bought a wire hanger, formed it into a tight loop at one end, and stuck it in through the top of the window. After about twenty or thirty minutes, the lock popped up and we were able to open the door of the van. No one had cell phones back then, so the only way to get a hold of anyone was to find a pay phone and dial the phone number, which, of course, we didn't know.

Terri and I, after some time had passed, pulled up and parked the van under the beach house that was built on stilts. We proceeded to unload the groceries. Granny stuck her head out the door and called to us, wondering where we had been. A little embarrassed to tell our story, we admitted what had happened and, also, how we had saved the day by our quick thinking regarding the coat hanger. Granny just shook her head and smiled as she helped us put things away. I wish we could say that we all had a nice bowl of ice cream that night, but unfortunately that was not the case.

Granny had a love for her family and enjoyed spending time with us in the summer. Our lives became intertwined throughout the years. She would visit us whenever she could. It was always nice to see her. Granny often came with us to the beach house. Sometimes, she would ride in our car. I would normally start the drive by sitting in the back. On this trip I was starting to feel car sick by the time we made it to the West Virginia Turnpike. The winding roads had a way of making me nauseous. Granny always carried clove gum in her handbag. We stopped the car so I could move to the front middle seat. Granny handed me a piece of gum and we were on our way.

I didn't mind sitting by my dad while he drove. I enjoyed looking at the map that he had stashed beside the seat. It was a challenge to keep up with the different towns we passed through. Dad pointed to where we were on the map and then to where we were going. Ugh, it seemed like it would take forever.

Mom could tell I was already getting bored. After we were through the mountains and I was feeling better, she handed me one of my favorite books to read to keep me entertained. It was called *Little Witch* by Anna Elizabeth Bennett. It was about a little girl who was raised as a witch's child only to find out that her true mother had been banished behind a looking glass by a spell that the witch had cast on her years before. I loved that book. It was quirky and fun, and I found myself laughing at the whimsical way the little girl in the story faced her problems. Once I finished reading it, I would go back to the beginning and read it all over again.

Mom brought Dad's metal thermos for the long drive. Before we left home, she made a pot of coffee to bring with us for Dad to drink along the way. When we stopped to switch my seat to the front so I wouldn't get sick, Mom poured him a fresh mug in his travel cup.

We had only been driving for a few minutes before I again was asking how much longer it would take before we got to the beach. I was sitting beside Dad and couldn't see his watch, so I asked him what time it was. Forgetting he had a cup of hot coffee in his hand, he proceeded to turn his wrist to see his watch. He was just about to spill his coffee into his lap when he caught himself just in time. Realizing what he had nearly done, he looked my way with wide eyes and smiled. I cracked up laughing at the thought of how close he came to the unpleasant mishap. My dad was good at making me smile. We had no trouble laughing at our silliness, and we both agreed that it would have been bad if he actually did spill his coffee. Mom, who was sitting beside me, looked up from her book and wondered what we were laughing about. I glanced back at Granny who saw the whole thing. She grinned and shook her head as she turned to look out her window.

I was glad that Granny had given me the gum. Granny, whom I had been sitting beside before I moved to the front seat, looked out her window as she sang her little song that she had taught me a while back.

"Kookaburra sits in the old gum tree…"[1]

I began to feel better, and I couldn't wait to get to the beach house. I was looking forward to spending more time with her. Granny and I shared the back bedroom where there were two twin beds, and we also shared the bathroom that was next to it.

Dad, Blaine, Bruce, and me on one of our Florida vacations

Granny was a good cook. I found myself watching her from the balcony that overlooked the kitchen in Snuggle Inn. Everyone in the family took turns with the cooking during the week. On Granny's night to cook, she made my favorite dish that she called pigs in a blanket, or cabbage rolls. One night while on vacation at the beach house, we had gone out to eat at one of the local restaurants. Later that night my stomach was upset. Granny could hear me as I tossed and turned in the bed next to hers. Granny went down to the kitchen and made me a drink of warm water with lemon juice. After sipping on the drink, I felt much better. Granny knew things like that. That's

---

[1] "Kookaburra," written by Marion Sinclair, 1932, Larrikin Music.

part of what made her such a good granny. She could always make things better. I enjoyed our conversations during that trip and others over the years. Granny was special, and I loved her very much.

Terri, me, Mom, Barb (Brian's wife), and Granny Kmetz
at the beach house Holden Beach, North Carolina

Forever Family

Each time we traveled, whether it was in Florida or North Carolina, the salt air was the first thing I noticed as our drive took us closer to the ocean. Such a distinct smell, not like the smells we have in Ohio. Standing on the back porch of the beach house, I took a deep breath as I stood smelling the salt air while looking toward the water. I had gathered my towel and my raft because I knew Brian was already riding the waves, and I looked forward to doing the same. Often, Brian and I would share the same raft. Other times, we would each ride our own and race to see who could make it to the shore first. He was the oldest of my brothers. I didn't have as many opportunities to spend time with Brian because of his work schedule. Vacationing as a family, we got to see each other more.

I watched Blaine, the middle of my three brothers, fly his kite. He motioned for me to come and help him. As I walked down the long boardwalk that connected the cottage to the beach, I watched him maneuver it, pulling on the string to keep it from falling. Occasionally, he would let me try. I followed his lead on how to do it as he coached me on the art of flying a stunt kite. He always wore a funny hat. Being a redhead, his skin burned easily, so he was rarely on the beach without it.

When I first came to live with the Pecks, Blaine took me out into the front yard. He handed me a rubber ball about the size of a soccer ball and told me to kick it so he could take my picture. So I kicked the ball. Snapping the picture at just the right time, he captured the moment. This was one of the first pictures taken of me when I came to live with the Pecks.

The first picture taken of me by my brother, Blaine,
when I went to live with the Pecks

I remember when Blaine knocked on my bedroom door one afternoon. He told me there was a treasure outside, but I had to go find it. Curious as to what he was talking about, I followed the directions he had given me on where to look. Following his instructions to a tee, I made my way to the front yard. Tall trees between the houses made good hiding spots when we played. Looking on the ground next to the biggest of the trees, as I had been directed, I came across what Blaine had described to me as "the treasure." Nestled between the tall blades of grass was something I had never held in my hand before. It wasn't a toy, like I had anticipated, but rather a feather. I picked it up, not quite sure if I was disappointed or excited. Deciding I was excited, I ran inside to show him.

Holding the feather up before me, pinched between my two fingers, I presented "the treasure." Smiling at me, he said, "Well done," and then he turned and walked away. That's how brothers are, you know.

Spending time with Blaine on the beach was no different, lots of shells to find, which he would point out as we walked along. We always had fun together. When he started dating Terri, I would follow them around everywhere. That soon ended when Mom told me to give them some space, which I reluctantly did.

When he got engaged to Terri, I still wanted to be with them. Terri was like the sister I never had. We were six years apart in age, but that didn't matter to us. We never went looking for trouble, but it seemed to find us. Some ideas were just too good to pass up. One time, Bruce was dating a girl I didn't like. She was, well, let's just say neither Terri nor I approved; we knew Bruce could do better!

Mom and Dad had gone away together on a cruise. Bruce was left home, and I stayed with Terri. We couldn't let a perfectly good night go by without checking on Bruce to see what trouble we could catch him in. We decided to drive by the house, and when we did, guess whose car was parked out front! I don't know which one of us came up with the idea to TP her car, but it was a good one!

We drove to the store and purchased enough toilet paper to do the job. As we pulled into the driveway, Terri turned off the headlights so they couldn't see us. I stood on one side of her car while Terri stood on the other. Carefully, we rolled the paper under the driver's door to the other side of the car and over the roof and again under the door and over the roof. We had that car so covered that we knew it would take some effort before she was able to find the handle to open the door. We found out that it's quite easy to toilet paper a car, and we got her good. We weren't expecting the rain that came that evening. We kind of felt bad about the mess she had to clean up. It wasn't long before Bruce broke up with her. When he found out we were the ones who decorated her car, he laughed and commended us on doing such a fine job.

*****

As a family, we traveled for several weeks during the summer, often staying at campgrounds. My favorite, next to the Yogi Bear Campground, was Assateague Island. The island is a thirty-seven-mile long barrier island located off the eastern coast of Delmarva. The northern two-thirds of the island is in Maryland while the southern third is in Virginia.

What I loved most about camping on this island were the wild ponies. Local folklore says the Assateague ponies are survivors of a shipwreck off the Virginia coast. The descendants of these ponies roam freely on the island. There are thought to be about three hundred ponies that are split into two main herds—one on the Virginia side and one on the Maryland side.

Ponies on the beach fascinated me. I took lots of pictures. My favorite was one I took of a mare and her foal—two of my favorite things, ponies and the ocean. Camping on Assateague Island was one of my best memories.

The ponies of Assateague Island

On one of our trips, Bruce and I went clamming. Working together, we made a good team. Bruce and I were closest in age, and we were always goofing off and teasing each other. He didn't like it when I called him "Brucie." He would chase me around the house until I locked myself in my room so he couldn't get to me. On this day, we got along fine and brought back to the campsite enough clams for Mom to make a big pot of clam chowder. It sure tasted good that night, and Bruce and I were proud to announce that dinner was because of us!

We often spent our days swimming at the beach, riding the waves on our rafts, and playing with the sand fleas. I loved to scoop them up in my hands as they burrowed down into the sand trying to get away. They tickled my palm as I played with them. When I was done, I would place them back on the wet sand so they could hide from the sandpipers, which would run back and forth dodging the waves trying to catch them for dinner. I would, at times, just sit and watch them.

The evenings were usually cooler than the days. Dad started a campfire as Mom got out the graham crackers, chocolate, and marsh-mallows so we could make s'mores. I loved to sneak and eat the choc-olate before even roasting the marshmallows. I was careful to keep the marshmallows away from the flames so as not to burn them. With a little help from an adult or one of my brothers, I eventually got one right. Making them might have been a challenge, but I had no trouble eating them. We also spent many camping trips at the Muskingum River in Ohio. Mom and Dad had good friends that owned property there. I loved to go camping—riding my bike during the day, hiking, swimming. At night, my brothers and I couldn't wait to roast hot dogs on long sticks and make fruit pies in little pie pans that we would push into the coals on the open fire.

We had a pop-up camper. It collapsed so we could pull it behind the car, and then, when we got to where we were going, Dad pulled the sides out and set it up. Inside, there was plenty of room. It had a stove and a small fridge and several areas to sleep. I got to sleep on one side that pulled out while Mom and Dad slept on the other. Blaine liked to sleep outside on the picnic table in his sleeping bag, which always seemed a little weird to me. Bruce and Brian slept in the other part of the camper.

With the screen windows unzipped all around me so I could feel the night air and smell the campfire, it was easy to sleep at night when we camped. Curled up in my sleeping bag, I could hear the crickets chirping all around and see the lightning bugs as they flew by. Mom and Dad talked quietly around the fire with their friends as it started to burn low; the campground was quiet. Good memories were being made, and I was very blessed to be where I was. Instead of me falling asleep to the cat clock in the playroom of Cole Cottage, I was now falling asleep to the sounds of my Mom and Dad talking while in the security of my forever family. God, yes! You can hear me!

Pearl

Dad, Blaine, Mom, Brian, and Grandma
Peck. My first Easter Sunday.

She sold Avon. Her name was Pearl, Grandma to me. Going to her house was like exploring the purse of my social worker, who would let me play with her lipsticks. Grandma Peck, Dad's mom, was soft-spoken, had the most beautiful skin, and could bake the most amazing pies.

Occasionally, I would spend the night at Grandpa and Grandma's house. Cuyahoga Falls was just twenty minutes or so from home, so we visited often. Packing my bag for a weekend visit, I knew I needed clothes for church on Sunday. Grandma always went, even though Grandpa didn't. I knew it was important to her. The houses and neighborhoods in Grandma's community were older. Neatly mani-cured lawns and beautiful streetlights lined the road. Pulling into the gravel driveway, we stopped just shy of the garage that sat detached from the house. The kitchen door was right there, so I unloaded my stuff and proceeded to knock.

Greeting us, Grandma Peck always seemed happy, even though, at times, she remained quiet during some discussions. I knew she was always a lady. Once, she had two of my cousins and me spend the night. During a spirited pillow fight, one of her favorite lamps got broken. I felt so bad; we all did. Grandma's look was one of disappointment, but she never got angry. She smiled at us and said, "These things happen sometimes." That day I realized how much more important we were to her than that lamp.

Heading into the house, I knew my way up the narrow stairs to the bedroom next to the bathroom. The windows were open. I placed my bag on the bed and looked out to the backyard. Grandpa had gone outside and was trying to feed the squirrels. He was bending over making a clicking noise with his tongue while trying to get the attention of a reluctant, but hungry, squirrel. His patience was amazing to me. As the squirrel got closer, Grandpa's clicking got louder. Eventually, the timid squirrel got up enough nerve to take the peanut out of his hand. I was fascinated by what I just saw. I hurried down the steps just as Mom was getting ready to leave. Quickly giving her a hug goodbye, I darted out the kitchen door so I could catch Grandpa before he came back inside. He handed me a peanut and showed me how to click my tongue so I too could feed one. Leaving me to my task, he headed back inside.

Mom was coming out the door while getting her keys out of her purse. As she walked toward the car, she said she would see me tomorrow. She backed out of the drive, and then she was gone.

It seemed like forever trying to get that squirrel to trust me. Giving up, I went back inside. "Maybe tomorrow," Grandma said. Grandpa looked over the top of his paper with a little grin on his face. The house was small but cozy. Grandma had set the table in the dining room with pretty plates and nice silverware. She always made things special. I know they enjoyed when I came to visit. I enjoyed it too.

Watching Grandpa eat fascinated me. Grandma Peck's cooking was always good, but no matter what she served, Grandpa would take the pepper shaker and proceed to cover his entire plate with the black seasoning. He seemed to love every bite he took. I couldn't help but wonder where this habit came from.

Dinner was over and the sun was setting. There's just something special about spending the night at Grandma's house. A feeling like I was someone very important. I knew they liked me being there. It was time for bed, so I climbed up the stairs. The room I was staying in was decorated beautifully. Every detail was thought through, from the beautiful comforter to the pretty lights on the nightstands. I felt like a princess when I slept there. It was a cool spring night. I looked out the window as the breeze gently blew the white sheer curtains. It was now dark, and the moonlight illuminated the room. I slid under the pretty comforter and placed my head on the crisp white pillow. Tomorrow was church. I had set my outfit on the chair, so everything was ready to go.

*****

Scrambled eggs with salt and a side of peanut butter toast were on the menu for breakfast. The toast not only had a thick layer of peanut butter, but Grandma also put a pad of real butter on first, which made it all the more creamy. I told her Mom didn't do that at home, to which she just smiled and said, "Oh." Grandma was never one to talk much about what other folks did or didn't do. She was polite that way. Breakfast was over and I was dressed and ready, curious about the makeup Grandma had upstairs. I asked if I could see it.

Stashed behind her reading chair in her sewing room was her sample makeup. The lipsticks normally came in a turquoise box, which usually contained about thirty lipstick samples. Grandma's samples were all in a plastic bag. These were the samples that she didn't need anymore, so she let me play with them. They were small, about an inch or two long, and I was in heaven!

Remembering back on the day when my social worker would let me play with her lipsticks, I knew this would be fun, except my plan was to use them on myself this time. Knowing we would be heading out the door any minute to go to church and knowing I had never been allowed to wear makeup before, I put on just a little—a light pink color on my lips and a very light red on my cheeks. I was so grown up; at least in my mind I was.

Grandpa didn't go to church very often but was happy to drop us off. Grandma never did learn to drive. The church was a few blocks away, so it didn't take long to get there. The church was very old, and I could see the big brick building and tall steeple as we approached the parking lot. After Grandpa dropped us off, we proceeded to walk up the paved steps and enter through two big white double wooden doors at the front of the church.

The hallway at the back of the church was long and dark. People were scurrying about placing their jackets on the hooks that were attached to the wall. The church was a busy place, so we quickly hung our jackets up on the hooks along with everyone else's, and then we entered the sanctuary to find our seats.

Grandma knew a lot of people. Many came up to say hello and give her a hug. After the pleasantries were over, most asked who I was, to which she proudly said, "This is Sandy, my granddaughter." Most made nice comments and referred to the fact that I was visiting for the weekend.

No one knew I was a foster child. No one knew that Grandma Peck was not my biological grandmother. One lady even commented on how much I looked like her. Grandma just smiled and shook her head in agreement, glancing at me and giving a quick wink. I was proud to be her granddaughter because I knew by her actions she loved me and she didn't want me to feel anything other than I was a part of her family.

The large pipe organ began to play, so we quickly took our seats. Reaching for the hymnal on the pew in front of me, I asked Grandma what page to turn to for our first song. The music echoed in the large ornate room. I watched the person who led the music at the front. He seemed to enjoy what he was doing as his hands moved up and down to the rhythm of the music.

Beautiful stained-glass windows lined the sanctuary, and I found myself studying them during the sermon. Each one told a story. Most of the stories I could make out because I had been attending Sunday school with my family. Jesus on the cross was one of the windows, and next to that He was ascending into heaven. The Easter story was special to me. I remembered getting dressed in my best dress at Cole Cottage to attend church on Easter Sunday. It was a special time, a happy time, and I had fond memories of celebrating it with my friends. Jesus had to die on the cross, we were taught, but He wasn't dead. He rose on the third day! Jesus did this because He loves us, and He wants us to live with him in heaven someday.

My mind drifted to my time when I attended church on Easter Sunday with the girls at Cole Cottage and to thoughts of my mother. I wonder where my mother was, my birth mother. I knew she had died when I was a baby. Did she go to heaven? Did she have a chance to visit a beautiful church like this one? Had she heard the good news of the Easter story? It seemed like the older I got, the more questions I had, and I wondered if they would ever be answered.

After church was over, Grandpa picked us up and brought us back to the house. Grandpa had spent his morning watching sports. We were all hungry, so lunch was served, and before I knew it, three o'clock rolled around. I gathered my things because I knew Mom would be here soon.

Heading back outside with a peanut in my hand, I once again tried to get that squirrel to trust me. Clicking my tongue and being patient finally paid off. The squirrel slowly approached and then quickly snatched it from me, darting up the tree. He stopped halfway up and turned around, hanging by his back feet while holding the nut with his front feet as he quickly devoured the special treat. Glad that I had not given up, I turned toward the kitchen door. Grandpa had been watching out the window and was laughing to himself as he turned to head back to his recliner in the living room.

I was talking to Grandma about the squirrel when Mom pulled up in the car. I picked up my overnight bag that I had brought down from the upstairs bedroom. I had tossed it onto a chair in the living room. I thought to myself how fast the visit had gone. Mom entered the front door and greeted us and thanked Grandma for having me over. Glancing my way, she quickly took me by the chin, "Are you wearing makeup?" Ah! I had forgotten I had it on. Not wanting her to see me like that, I intended to take it off before she arrived. "She didn't go to church like that, did she?" As my eyes widened, I glanced over at Grandpa sitting in his recliner. He sheepishly slid down in his chair, pretending to hide behind his paper.

Grandma smiled at Mom and, without hesitation, said, "Oh, no, she was just playing with my samples." Looking relieved, Mom paused, studied my face, and then instructed me to get my things. I gathered up my bag as Mom and Grandma talked about the day's events. I had fun visiting my grandparents and looked forward to doing it again. As we started toward the door, I gave Grandma a big hug goodbye. She squeezed me tight and again winked at me. The makeup was our little secret. Grandma hadn't realized I had worn the makeup to church; she honestly didn't think twice about it. She knew I meant no harm, and it wasn't worth the effort to explain what I had done. I just knew that someday when I grew up, I wanted to be a grandma just like her.

The Lie

Of all the things I did in the summer, riding my bike was what I enjoyed doing most. By now I was in junior high, or middle school as it's called now. I was old enough to venture out on my own. The church we used to attend was in Uniontown. I knew the way well. I would often go on long bike rides. As long as I let Mom know where I was going, she only required me to attach the tall bright orange safety flag to the back of the bike so cars could see me as I rode.

It was early afternoon; I threw some money in my pocket and yelled goodbye as I ran out the back of the house through the mud room door. Quickly unlocking the shed, I pulled out the bike from beside the mower. I was now big enough to ride my brother's twelve-speed bike. It was a great day for a ride. There was no sign of rain, and it wasn't too hot, at least not yet. I pushed the end of the flag into the mount that was already attached, hopped on, and rode across the backyard to the side that led to the front.

The trip was about ten miles. Starting out on Robinwood, the road curved and turned into Frawood. The main road was Raber. I would follow that road for most of the way. Turning right onto Raber, I began to pedal fast. The houses on the left side of Raber were set back from the road.

Behind those houses was a hill that we used for sled riding in the winter. The one house that I always strained to see when we drove past was the one with the white fence that led up to a small barn. There was always a white horse in the fenced area and no other animals around. I was curious if anyone ever rode that horse. As I pedaled by, I again strained to catch a look at the beautiful white horse.

The country club was to my right. My neighbor, Shannon, and her family had bought a house there and moved a few years back. I didn't see much of her anymore; I had been selfish when it came to being happy for her. It seemed to me that she only wanted to talk about her fancy new house and all the stuff she had. It's sad how I allowed something so petty to divide a friendship, but I did. Pedaling faster now, anticipating the hill I was approaching, I noticed the golf course was busy today. Dad often golfed there, but we weren't members. Farther down the road was a big gold and green sign that read, "Prestwick." I never rode my bike there because I couldn't get in. Cars would have to stop and show ID before they could enter.

Coming to the four-way stop, I caught my breath and waited as the cars took their turns at the intersection. Another mile down the road was Lori's house. We were still good friends, although getting older now. We no longer called each other Clark Bar and Coleslaw. We enjoyed spending time together. My family started going to a new church the year before, but we still saw each other at school and occasionally on the weekends.

Kreighbaum Road was the next turn after Lori's house. Around the corner and across the road from Lori's house was a farm. The farm almost always had horses in the front corral. I had such a love for horses. The days I played at Lori's house she knew I was going to ask if we could walk across the street and pet them. One visit, we walked over to feed them. After the horse that I was feeding devoured the handful of grass I had given him, he suddenly moved his head in a funny way and let off the biggest sneeze I had ever seen. Shocked by the quick explosion, my once clean shorts and T-shirt were now covered in the slimy chewed up grass. Lori, who had been standing a few paces down the fence, couldn't stop laughing. "Glad he didn't sneeze on me," she said, still standing there with my arms out to my side as I assessed the mess. I couldn't believe what had just happened. I guess if the horse would have sneezed on her I would have responded the same way she did. Thinking back, I recalled the conversation I had with Mom, as I explained to her what had happened the next day when she did my laundry.

*****

Outdoors was our playground. Whether it was summer or winter, we were always finding something to do. This farmer's property was also where my brother Bruce broke his leg. We had gone sled riding with Lori and some friends. Someone had brought a car hood to use as a sled. Bruce coaxed me to ride down with him. He was in the back and I sat in front of him. Halfway down the hill we knew we were heading for a group of trees. With nowhere else to go and no way to stop the hood, Bruce knew we were going to crash. Knowing I would get the brunt of the blow when we hit, Bruce pushed me off the hood onto the path as he continued to plow head-on into the trees.

I don't know how we got him back up the hill and to the hospital with a broken leg, but I was thankful for his quick thinking. He spent many weeks healing from that decision and people couldn't help but ask the question, "Why? Why a car hood?" Sometimes there are really no good answers.

I smiled as I remembered the good times we had. I passed Lori's house and continued to pedal my way along the winding road. I stopped to catch my breath at the end of the driveway of one of Mom's friends. Her name was Ruth. She was my mom's consultant on homeopathic treatments for nearly everything. On occasion, when I was out running errands with Mom, we would stop by Ruth's house to get her vitamins.

Ruth's property had large trees and lots of flowers. The driveway was long and curved around to the back of the house where it divided the main house from another house where Ruth stored her supplies. Next to the house was a pond with a fountain in the middle. Several canoes were flipped upside down next to the cattails, waiting for someone to use them. Ruth had hired Bruce to do work around her property. The house was older and there were a lot of flower beds to weed. She kept him busy all summer. My break now over, I was ready to get on my way. I pedaled past Ruth's house and was able to coast partway before the road took a turn and I had to start pedaling again. By the time I had made it to the church, about an hour had passed since I left my house. I was thirsty, so I stopped at a drugstore, pulled some change out of my pocket, and bought a pop. That's what we call a soda in Ohio. Sitting on the cement step that led up to the drugstore, I pulled the metal top off the can and pushed it back through the open hole.

The church driveway was a few yards away, just next door. The afternoon sun was hot. While I sat there drinking my ice-cold beverage, I was reminded of the time everyone from our old church went Christmas caroling around the small town. Mom and Dad had been the youth leaders for several years when we attended there. One evening before Christmas, all the kids that were a part of the youth group and some of their friends bundled up and headed out for a night of fun and fellowship. Even though it was freezing, we spread Christmas cheer to all who could withstand the cold long enough for a line or two of "Away in a Manger."

Fond thoughts of that special night came back to my memory. The sidewalks had been beautifully lit by the streetlights as we walked from house to house while big flakes of snow slowly fell. Looking back, the memory reminds me of a Thomas Kinkade painting that I had seen. *What I wouldn't give for some of that cooler air today*, I thought. Finishing my pop, I let out a big belch that I thought would make my brothers proud. Tossing the empty can into the trash, I got back on my bike.

The town was nice to ride through. There was an old building that was being used as a bakery. In the past, we would often stop there Sunday afternoons after church to get some fresh baked goods. The town consisted of mostly residences, although there were a few businesses, like the bakery and the drugstore. It was a workday, so lots of people were coming and going.

Knowing Mom would worry if I stayed too long, I headed back the way I came. Most of the ride was shaded, but the sections where it wasn't could get rather hot in the late afternoon sun. I was almost home and was just about to turn down Frawood when, again, the curiosity of the white horse made me glance that way. I coasted to a stop, put down the kickstand, and maneuvered my bike beside the big evergreen tree that marked the spot where we usually stood as we waited for the school bus. While I waited for traffic to pass so I could cross the street, I noticed the horse grazing at the far end of the yard.

Intending only to pet her, I innocently proceeded to the fence. She was beautiful, even though her mane hadn't been combed and was somewhat knotted. Clicking my tongue like my grandpa taught me, I called for the mare. She ignored me, so I decided to tempt her with some grass from the other side of the fence. Seeing what I was doing quickly got her attention. Putting my foot on the first rail of the fence, I greeted her as she approached. Eagerly, she took the grass from my hand. I was hoping I wouldn't get sneezed on. Getting to pet the horse I had so longed to visit was a perfect end to an already perfect day. You would think that I would have been happy with that.

I was there for quite a while. No one came out of the house to ask what I was doing or to offer me a ride. They were probably working; apparently no one was home. Taking the next step on the rail of the fence, I thought to myself, *It's a small fenced area. I would be okay just walking her around.* Making perfect sense to me, I convinced myself to throw my leg over and ride bareback. I thought I could take a quick ride and then hop on my bike and head home in time for supper.

There was a reason I never saw anyone riding the beautiful white horse. As soon as my butt hit her back, she bolted. Grabbing her mane and squeezing my legs as tight as I could, I held on for dear life. She was fast, but there was nowhere to go. She was contained within the white fence. Charging fast, she headed around the pen toward the area where I had been standing. Blocked by the fence and unable to go any further, she came to an abrupt halt.

Like some old slow motion Western, I found myself being hurled off her back. I tried to keep a tight rein on her mane, but I just couldn't do it. I hit the fence hard. Landing beside her, I couldn't believe what I had just done. I stood up quickly and looked around to see if anyone saw me, but no one was around. The pain in my left arm was bad. I grabbed it with my right and cradled it, hoping that would help. What had I done? Why didn't I just keep riding my bike until I got home? How was I going to explain this one?

I walked quickly across the road, holding my arm close to my chest. I got on my bike and headed home. Once inside the shed, I leaned the bike against the side, not caring if it fell. The back door to the mud room was open so I quietly went in. I was hoping Mom wouldn't see me. I cut through the living room down the hall to my bedroom and closed the door.

Looking in my mirror, I could see a few scratches mainly on my arms where they impacted the fence. I was a little dirty and sweaty. I looked at my arm; it looked fine but it hurt badly. I could move it okay, so it couldn't be broken, right? Maybe it will be okay.

Not saying a word about the fall, I spoke only of the fun I had on my bike ride as we finished dinner. Mom noticed that something was wrong. "What's wrong?" she asked.

How would I explain this? I either had to fess up and tell the truth or come up with one heck of a lie. "I fell off my bike today!" What? Did I just lie? Of course I did. I couldn't imagine the trouble I would get in if I told the truth. After all, I will be fine in a day or two and no one will ever know. Or so I thought.

The pain continued through the evening. If I just get a good night's rest, I will be fine tomorrow. Mom had given me some ice to keep on it as I propped it up on my spare pillow. Falling asleep was hard, but I eventually fell asleep only to wake up a short time later. I was up most of the night. The first thing in the morning, I asked my mom if I could have something for the pain. By now my arm was swollen and beginning to turn black and blue. "That must have been some wipeout on your bike," she said. "I think you need to see a doctor."

X-rays showed a hairline fracture. "You need to be more careful riding your bike," the doctor said as he placed a soft cast on my arm. I didn't know how to respond to that. I wasn't about to tell anyone the truth, so I said nothing. I had learned my lesson. I paid dearly with the pain I suffered. I would never ride a horse I didn't know ever again. Unfortunately, I didn't learn my lesson about lying. I kept that secret, not telling anyone for many years.

*My best friend, Lori, and me the summer
I broke my arm riding the horse*

What's in a Name?

My parents continued to manage my behavior, and they took full advantage of the opportunities that SCCS had provided. Before long, a plan had been established for me to remain in my home with the Peck family indefinitely.

"Mrs. Cole!" Not knowing her name was Mrs. Peck, my friend, Lisa, who lived across the street, kept trying to get my mom's attention. This happened a lot. Friends would come over, knowing my last name was Cole, and they would mistakenly call Mom by my last name. Having to explain over and over again, Mom could see I was getting frustrated and a little embarrassed. I didn't want to have to go through the whole story every time I invited someone over.

"Her name is Mrs. Peck," I would say again and again. Mom contacted Children's Services to check into changing my name. I was thirteen when the Summit County Court of Common Pleas officially changed my name to Sandra Jean Peck.

They were excited to tell me. Mom and Dad took me aside, handed me the paper, and waited for me to read it. Looking it over twice, I glanced up at them. I was grinning from ear to ear as they waited for my response. I remembered the prayer I had prayed long ago when I had visited the home where the older kids, who had been waiting for their forever home, lived: *"God, if you're listening, please don't let me end up here!"* I couldn't help but feel overwhelmed at the thought that this was the final step in making me a permanent part of this family. I was never adopted; that would have required contact with my birth father, and there was no need to ask him. As far as I was concerned, the Pecks were my family. I no longer wondered if I would stay or be sent back to the children's home. This finalized the whole process. Mom said, "Now you don't have to explain why my name is different from yours." I was happy. My new name sounded different to me as it rolled off my tongue but not in a bad way. This was a true act of love, and I really appreciated what my parents had done.

*****

My parents were very encouraging to me when it came to my past. They knew I had vivid memories, so they suggested to me that they could contact the children's home and inquire about my mother's grave site. Within a few weeks, we found out where she was buried.

It was a fall day. I was anxious to know more about my past from a social worker who had come to pick me up. As we drove to Hillside Memorial, I thought about how close my mother was all along. The park was located on Canton Road near Springfield Lake, not far from my house. We turned into the cemetery. There were many large trees and rolling hills. The headstones were not visible; they were flat, so maintaining the grounds would be easier. I could see the occasional flower arrangement propped up lovingly beside the plots that had been recently visited. A large church building was to the right, beside the property. Between the church building and the rolling hills of headstones was a large beautiful white angel statue. She was standing with her arms out in front of her; her wings were stretched out, giving almost a sense of embrace. Her head was tilted down as she looked longingly into the eternal flame that was burning within the palms of her hands. Continuing our drive along the long, winding path past the rows of headstones, I watched until I couldn't see it any longer.

Trees lined the long path. The leaves were beginning to change, and some had fallen to the ground. I could hear them crunch under the tires of the car as we drove. Winding our way through the grounds up over the hill and toward the back, we finally came to a stop. I opened the car door and got out. I noticed a chain-link fence that seemed to be the boundary that divided the cemetery and the adjoining neighborhood. "It's right over there," she said as the social worker unfolded the map she had been given.

On the other side of the fence were two dogs sunning themselves in the adjacent neighborhood. As soon as they heard us, they began to bark while running back and forth the length of the fence. Fortunately, they soon lost interest. As I walked in the direction I was told to go, I slowly shuffled through the fallen leaves. Each step I took stirred up that earthy, musty smell that comes from dead, wet leaves that haven't been raked. I began to read each headstone, feeling a bit anxious as I searched. I finally found the one I was looking for. I took a deep breath. In a strange sort of way, I felt as if I was being introduced to someone I was only told about. She *was* real, and I felt like I was meeting her for the very first time. I knelt beside the marker, brushed the dry leaves away, and read what was engraved.

Mother and Daughter
Phyllis J. Cole
February 2, 1943–May 13, 1965

I was so thankful to finally see where Mother was buried. It brought closure, but at the same time it opened up a whole new curiosity for me. She was so young. She didn't even have a chance to enjoy being a mommy to me. Right then a strong breeze blew and some of the dry fallen leaves danced around me as a shiver went up my back from the blast of the cool air. I stood up, pulled the front of my jacket closed, and zipped it. The wind was beginning to pick up; I could tell a storm was brewing, so we shuffled our way back through the fallen leaves. Driving down the hill, we once again passed the white angel. The sky was now gray and drops of rain danced on the hood of the car. The social worker reached for the switch to turn on the wipers. They squeaked across the glass as they moved back and forth. I was lost in thought. What other information about my past is out there? What else could I find out? I still had so many unanswered questions. Unfortunately, that was all I was going to know, at least for now.

It was getting late and I had to get home. Tonight, I had my Bible study meeting with the youth group at church. The church we were now attending had lots of programs for kids my age. Middle school students were in a group called the Alphateens, and the high school students were called the Omegateens. The groups were named based on the Bible verse found in Revelation 22:13, "I am the Alpha and the Omega, the first and the last, the beginning and the end" (NASB). The leaders of the youth group, Stan and Joyce Gibbs, were a wonderful couple. They had kids of their own in the youth group, so they wanted to help contribute in some way to the ministry. Sunday nights was when the groups met.

Mom and Dad had given me a Bible for Christmas. I was thirteen at the time. It was leather and had indentations on the pages where each book of the Bible began, which made it easier to look up verses. On the inside cover, my parents wrote:

> *Dear daughter, we know you will continue to grow in Christ as you read the Word. You will be smoothed and perfected if you allow God to work in your life. Remember to pray for His guidance in all things.*
>
> *Love,*
> *Mom and Dad, Christmas 1978*

This Bible, unlike my first Bible, was for someone older. I began attending youth group, and each meeting I would bring my Bible.

I admired Stan and Joyce. They showed their love for Jesus in the way they taught and the way they treated each teen. Some days, for me, were harder than others; I guess I was easy to read. Stan and Joyce often would ask how I was doing, sensing when I needed guidance. Always kind and encouraging, they would eventually cheer me up and I would feel better. Being a teenager has its challenges, and I had plenty of my own. Peer pressure, boys, my classes at school…the list goes on. Attending youth group, I heard solid teaching that built upon the lessons I had learned at an earlier age. Eager to learn more, I was faithful in attending most of the events that were scheduled.

The Pumpkin House was one of my favorite things we did as a church in the fall. Ohio was big on haunted houses. Some organizations in the Akron area would fix up old buildings and charge a fee for anyone who was looking for a good scare. Wanting another option for families, the church organized the Pumpkin House.

At the far end of the church building was the activity center. It was configured as a gym with basketball hoops and a stage. It was also located next to the kitchen. Although the youth in the church were usually the ones there on Sunday afternoons, it was also used for weddings and banquets. It was a great place to decorate for tours through the Pumpkin House. In place of scary stories, Bible stories were acted out as individual groups toured the fellowship hall. There was no charge to get in, only donations of canned goods for the local food bank.

Big drapes of white paper over fishing line divided the room; each smaller room had a different Bible story. Escorted by a tour guide, small groups of people, young and old, would weave their way back and forth through the maze of rooms, eventually making their way down the long hallway to the sanctuary.

Getting to the church early to change into my costume, I was eager to lead my first group. I had worked hard with my friends to organize the Pumpkin House. I was excited to see the looks on the little kids' faces. I was ready to go. Wide eyed, one little girl asked, "Is it scary?" Taking her by the hand as I knelt down beside her, I explained to her that it was dark but there were lights to show each Bible story, and at the end when we got to the sanctuary, there were cookies. Smiling, she seemed to accept my answer as her parents smiled back at me.

I enjoyed working with the little ones. I was thirteen, and God was working on my heart. I already had a love for serving. We walked through the large divided room and visited each story. The little girl held my hand while I told her how Jonah was swallowed by the whale and later obeyed God and how Jesus called for Zaccheus to come out of the sycamore tree. Each scene had members of the church acting out the story.

Our tour ended with the most precious scene of all—Baby Jesus, Mary, and Joseph. It wasn't Christmas; why end with that? The goal of the Pumpkin House was to give the families who didn't want to go to something scary a family-friendly event to celebrate the season. Of all the stories in the Bible, the story of Jesus was most important.

The sanctuary was quiet. When the tour was over, each group was invited to sit and pray or exit to the left where everyone was gathering for cookies. Letting go of my hand, the little girl looked up at me and said, "Thank you," and followed her parents to where the cookies were. Passing some of the other teens who were also tour guides, I headed back down the hall to get my next group.

I knew all the stories that had been acted out by members of the church as I escorted the little kids through the Pumpkin House. They were nice stories, but that's all they were. They weren't real, were they? I attended church every weekend with my family. I brought my Bible. I had lots of friends. I sang in the church's youth musical group; we were called the Omegateen Singers. We would travel and perform. All the girls in the group even had matching dresses. That said a lot about how good we were. God must be very pleased! Still, for me, something was missing. I often wondered, *Could God really love me like I was taught in Sunday school? What do I need to do to go to heaven? Am I a good enough person, or do I have to do more?* In the midst of my uncertainties and doubts, my questions were about to be answered.

Incredible Favor

The smell of French toast soon filled my bedroom. It was Sunday morning. I rubbed my eyes trying to wake up. I had been out late the night before with friends from the youth group. Our Saturday night bowling league usually didn't end until late. I wasn't very good at bowling but would surprise the members on my team with an occasional good score. I slowly shoved the bed covers to the side and allowed my feet to hit the floor. Rummaging through my closet, I picked out the dress I wanted to wear to church. I knew the dress would look nice with the higher-than-my-normal, ankle-wrap shoes Mom had surprised me with the week before. Glancing in the mirror, I approved of the way the outfit came together. I twirled around and headed down the hall toward the smell of the French toast that was coming from the kitchen

Mom had already prepared breakfast for everyone and was now working on the pot roast that would be finished cooking by the time we got home. The aroma of the slow-cooked meal made the house smell so good. We would be hungry, so it was nice to have lunch waiting for us when we returned home.

The morning rush was on; everyone was in a hurry to get out the door. We arrived in time to make it to Sunday school. When we first started attending Sunday school, I didn't always enjoy it. I mostly watched the clock while I sat with my friends in the small room that was used for my age group. I was respectful during that teaching time. I didn't always understand what was being taught, and I was too shy to ask questions. I had heard some of these passages of scripture before. When the topic of sin came up, I thought to myself, *I'm a good person. I go to church. What more do I have to do?*

After the Sunday school hour was over, we headed to the sanctuary. The sanctuary was large and was located central to the building. The seating was four sections of long, cushioned pews divided by three aisles, two on either side and one down the middle. The tall ceiling was made of wood beams, and spaced throughout were long hanging lights that were dimmed once the service began.

Directly behind the podium was a tall group of stained-glass windows. The light coming from behind the windows illuminated each piece of glass, sending the colors streaming down into the choir loft, which sat directly in front of it. There were five colorful windows in all. The main picture at the center of the windows was of Jesus standing with his arms open wide. Many Sunday mornings I would daydream while staring at that stained glass.

Each week the choir sang while being accompanied by the grand piano and organ that sat to the side of the pulpit. The melody of the two instruments would leave an echo throughout the room as the last note was played.

Some Sundays I sang in the choir. Occasionally, I volunteered in the nursery. When I wasn't singing in the choir or helping in the nursery, I sat with all the other students on the left side of the sanctuary. I admit, some Sundays my mind wandered as I thought more about what I was going to do after church rather than giving my full attention to the day's message.

My family and I had been attending Manchester Trinity Chapel for several years now. I was getting older, and God was beginning to reveal to me a new understanding of my sin and His holiness.

I don't remember the exact date; I wish I did. I do know I was fourteen. I was sitting with my friends in our usual seats. The choir had just finished the songs that were normally sung right before the message. Sitting down in the pews, my friends and I stashed our hymnals in the hymnal rack located on the back of the seats in front of us. The pastor instructed the congregation to take out their Bibles. The room was quiet except for the fluttering sound that the pages made as everyone turned to the passage we were about to study.

John 3:16 was the verse I had memorized so long ago. "For God so loved the world, that He gave His only begotten Son, that whoever believes in Him shall not perish, but have eternal life."

I listened as the pastor continued to teach from God's Word. That morning my mind was more focused on what was being taught. I turned to the passages of scripture that were being read. A feeling of conviction came over me. As I continued to listen, I had to come to terms with what God's Word was saying.

I had always wondered about heaven, questioning in the past if my mother went there when she died. I had always hoped she had. I was taught that it was an eternal place, a beautiful place, and I wanted to go too. Glancing around the room, I spotted my parents sitting on the other side. I did believe in God. I knew who He was. Was that enough? Remembering how I had always loved the Easter story, I grasped the significance of what Jesus had done on the cross.

For the first time, the message became clear. I was a sinner and separated from God. "For all have sinned and fall short of the glory of God" (Rom. 3:23 NASB). But God, in His mercy, made it possible for us to have eternal life. "For the wages of sin is death, but the free gift of God is eternal life in Christ Jesus our Lord" (Rom. 6:23 NASB). All who accept the gift God has provided through the death and resurrection of Jesus Christ will escape spiritual death.

> If you confess with your mouth Jesus as Lord, and believe in your heart that God raised Him from the dead, you will be saved; for with the heart a person believes, resulting in righteousness, and with the mouth he confesses, resulting in salvation. (Rom. 10:9–10 NASB)

God was drawing me, and now I was ready to respond.

The service was coming to a close. I could tell that the verses we read that morning had not only touched my heart but others as well. The room was quiet, and the music was reflective. Before the song ended, our pastor invited anyone who had questions or wanted someone to pray with them to come forward and meet at the front.

My heart was now beating faster. I felt as if everyone sitting by me could hear it. I knew that day that if I were to die, even though I knew what the Bible said and knew the answers to some of the questions in Sunday school, I would not go to heaven. I still had not talked to Jesus personally through prayer. I knew He had died for me on the cross, and I knew I had to believe and ask for forgiveness. Jesus was calling me into a relationship with Him. I was beginning to understand.

I felt as if my feet were glued to the floor. One by one, people started to walk forward. Bowing my head, I wanted to go… "Jesus, I know you love me… Please forgive me. Help me!" Looking up, I took the first step and started for the aisle. I didn't look at anyone except the pastor. He watched me approach, smiled, reached out his hand, and gave my shoulder a quick pat. He then turned and greeted another person who had made their way to the altar.

Bowing my head, I pretended there was no one else in the room. As I stood with the others who came forward, the choir sang one more verse. After the closing prayer, I wiped the tears from my face. Feeling someone behind me, I turned to see Mom and Dad and my brothers standing with me. As soon as I had walked to the front, they walked up too. I wasn't alone. They had prayed for me and encouraged me ever since I had moved in with them when I was seven, and now they were happy that I had made the most important decision of my life, and I was too.

When we become believers in Christ, we are changed. Our desires change. We want to serve and honor Him. It's not just about saying a prayer! It's about a relationship with the Creator, believing in His promises, trusting in His faithfulness, and relying on His Word.

When I first trusted in Christ, I never would have imagined how He would demonstrate His faithfulness to me, but I would soon learn that He can do much more than I could ever ask or imagine.

The Letter

Several weeks had passed since that Sunday morning. Even though my past was a mystery to me and I still had questions, there was a peace that I had never felt before. I was a part of something greater than myself. I now had an assurance that one day I would be with Jesus in heaven. Nothing could take that away from me. I was told there would be a baptism service scheduled soon. I knew that was the next step in professing my faith, so I let my parents know that I wanted to be baptized.

It was a cold day in November, a Saturday afternoon. It had been snowing for most of the day, so I decided to watch TV with my brothers. Mom was busy sewing a new outfit for Christmas when the doorbell rang. Keeping Duchess from barking, I picked her up as Dad got up to answer the door. A few minutes passed and I heard my parents talking to someone. Curious, I put Duchess down and walked through the living room to see what was going on. Standing on the front porch was a dark-haired man. As soon as he saw me, his face lit up. "It *is* you!" he exclaimed. My first instinct was to try and remember if I had done something wrong. I looked at Mom and tried to figure out if she was upset or just as puzzled as I was.

"Sandy, this is your uncle," my dad explained. Now I was really confused. I didn't recognize him. He wasn't my Uncle Gary that I used to live with. I looked at Dad; he looked at me. For a split second, visions from the movie *Annie* came to my mind when the counterfeit mom and dad came to claim Orphan Annie as their own, trying to swindle money from Big Daddy Warbucks.

"I know it's you; you have your daddy's eyes, and I see the scar on your right eyebrow from the car accident you were in with your grandmother when you were three." Convinced he knew something,

Dad invited him in. As he began to explain how he found me, I couldn't believe what I was hearing. When Dad first opened the door, he introduced himself and asked, "Does Sandy Cole live here?" I was no longer going by my birth last name; it had been almost a year since it was changed from Cole to Peck.

"Your grandmother sent me here to see if it was you. I received this letter in the mail a few days ago." He held up the letter for us to see. It was a band letter addressed to "The Parents of Sandy Cole." It had my name and address, and it led him straight to me. The really strange part was that nowhere on the letter did it have my uncle's address, yet it ended up delivered to his house. The only thing that was the same was that his last name was Cole. The year prior, the school had been notified of my name change, so why the letter had my birth name on it puzzled me. "Your grandmother has been wondering for years if you were okay and if you were happy. She never got to say goodbye. She was heartbroken, not knowing where you were."

It was all happening so fast. I too had wondered about my grandmother. I had so many memories, detailed memories. I didn't think I would ever see her again. How could this happen? He began to explain that my grandmother still lived in the same house I had lived in when I was three. Grandma's house wasn't far from where I now lived. How could a letter with my birth name and current address end up being delivered to my uncle's house? I felt a wave of excitement come over me. I was now fourteen. I hadn't seen my grandmother since I was four. Now what?

Mom took down his information and suggested my grandparents come for a visit. Plans were made to meet two weeks after Christmas. My uncle left, thanking my parents for allowing him to see and talk with me. They had every right to turn him away, but they didn't.

Afterward, I was sitting on the edge of my bed. My head was spinning, thinking of what had just happened, when Mom knocked on my bedroom door. She opened my door and came in with her Bible in hand. "I wanted to share this verse with you; I think it might be appropriate for what just happened." She handed me her Bible, and I read the verse she had highlighted, "Delight yourself in the Lord; And He will give you the desires of your heart" (Ps. 37:4 NASB).

At the time my mom gave me this verse, I thought that God had given me the desire of my heart, which was to understand my past. Instead, He gave me so much more—He gave me my family and answered so many of my questions.

As I have grown in my understanding of this verse, I have come to realize that it's not about God granting my human desires, although He certainly did when He led my family to me. It's about God manifesting His desires in my heart.

I still had questions, like: Why did my mother die? What was I like as a baby? Where were my grandmother and my other relatives?

Even though, when I was younger, I had dealt with some serious anger issues. Now that I was older, the anger was gone. People sometimes asked me why I wasn't angry, especially at God. I didn't understand why they thought I should be. All of these years when things didn't go my way—my mother dying, my father in Mansfield State Reformatory, the accident, moving from place to place, health problems, behavioral problems, and many unanswered questions—God was pulling the threads of my life into a beautiful tapestry, a colorful cloth that only a Master could weave. I knew there was a purpose for all of this. He loved me. My story was now beginning to unfold.

Grandma's Prayer

Mom had made some refreshments. We had already taken down the Christmas tree and decorations. My grandparents would be here any minute. My mind was reeling with questions. I was curious to see my family; it had been a long time since we last saw one another or even spoke. Looking out the window, I saw the car pull into the driveway. There was still snow on the ground, but Dad had made sure the front sidewalk was clear.

Watching as they got out of the car, I noticed there were four people. Holding the door open and greeting everyone with a smile, Mom introduced herself and Dad as they entered. I felt awkward as all eyes were on me. Taking their coats, Mom invited them to sit in the living room.

My grandmother was smiling as she reached out for me. She hugged me tight. I was now much taller than her. "I'm so glad to see you! You're so grown up!" I have never had a hug so tight; it seemed she would never let go. As we proceeded to the white couch, Grandma sat by me. Realizing I hadn't really acknowledged the other three people, I looked around the room. My grandpa and two uncles were just as curious to see me as Grandma was. Grandpa was just like I remembered him—still wearing his blue jean overalls and a baseball hat. He smiled at me and shot me a toothless grin. My uncles, now grown, were quiet as they kindly let Grandmother do the talking.

As we began our conversation, there was so much to tell and so much to hear. This was all new to me. She was telling me things I had never known and some things that I remembered exactly like she was explaining. As she began to tear up, I couldn't help but get a lump in my throat. "I had made a promise to your mother before she died that I would look after you, and when you were taken from me, it just about killed me. Not only did I lose my daughter, but I lost you too. Every Christmas I would pray. I would set up your little Christmas tree and wonder if you were happy, wonder if you were with a nice family. The only thing I ever wanted for Christmas was to know you were okay, and now look, two weeks after Christmas, my prayer has been answered."

Swallowing hard, I couldn't hold back the tears. Memories came flooding back. We laughed and cried as we talked. I asked her questions while telling her how I remembered living with her and how I remembered getting into the accident, how I lived with Aunt Carol and about my time at the children's home. She told me she wanted to come and see me but was told it would be better for me if she didn't. She mentioned how I wouldn't eat, saying it was the only thing I could control in my world that was so out of control. She knew back then that I needed help and my natural family just couldn't provide it.

The day I saw my Grandma Cole two weeks
after Christmas when I was fourteen

What about my father? Where was he? "We don't see much of him. He got remarried and 'got religion.'" I wasn't sure what that term meant. Grandma was a little bit country, so I had to pay close attention to what she was trying to say.

"You look like you got it real good here. Seems everything worked out best. I'm just glad you're okay." The conversation continued for another hour when she said they best be going. We made plans to visit and said our goodbyes, followed by another long hug.

As I helped Mom clean up the dishes, we talked. What an amazing story. I could never have orchestrated a story like this in my wildest imagination. Tired and mentally drained, I said good night and went to my room. As I prayed before falling asleep, the prayer was no longer, "God are you there?" or "God if you're listening" or "God please help!" It was a prayer of gratitude to an all-knowing, loving Creator who, all along, was helping, guiding, and protecting me when I was too young to do it myself. I looked forward to my visit at Grandma's house.

It wasn't long before we had that visit. I was excited to see if my memory matched up with the real thing. A short drive to Grandma's house and soon those questions would be answered. Twelve years later, I recognized the house right away. Mom drove up the long dirt driveway that led to the house, stopping just short of the garage. Feeling like I was stepping back in time, I took it all in. As she came out through the kitchen door, still drying her hands with a towel, Grandma smiled and greeted us.

The outside of the house and garage had not changed from what I remembered. I held the door as we entered the kitchen. It seemed smaller—the ceilings were low, and the only way we could walk into the dining room was single file. The wood-burning stove had been replaced with a more efficient electric unit, and the wallpaper had been replaced with wood paneling. "You fellers have a seat," she said. We enjoyed the afternoon as we talked. She brought out pictures. I had never seen a baby picture of myself. The only picture I had was one of my parents cutting their wedding cake.

As the day came to an end, I felt closer to my grandmother than ever before. She really did love me and my mother. I understood so much more than I ever have regarding the circumstances of my life. There was still so much to talk about, but it was getting late. I had school the next day, so we had to leave. Before leaving, I asked Grandma if I could use the bathroom.

"Sure, Sandy. Don't you remember? It's out back!"

The Uninvited Guest

I was learning more and more about my past. I enjoyed visits to my grandmother's house. Each visit she would invite someone in the family who was anxious to see me. Aunts, uncles, cousins—I didn't remember them, but they remembered me.

Grandma usually provided lunch—bologna sandwiches and some chips. Watching my grandpa eat a bologna sandwich was almost as painful for me to watch as it was for him to eat. Bite after bite, I would watch as he somehow managed to eat the entire sandwich with no teeth.

"I don't usually eat too much," Grandpa said. "It just hurts my stomach something fierce."

"Grandpa," I said, "it would be better for you if you put your teeth in once in a while!" He knew I was right. He looked at me and chuckled and then proceeded to grab a handful of chips.

Visiting Grandma Cole at her house. I was fifteen.

Grandpa Cole in his bib overalls and toothless grin. This picture was taken by me on one of my many visits when I was a teen.

I spent lots of time listening to my uncles, the ones who lived with me when I lived with Grandmother. They talked about my mother, how I looked like her, but I had my father's eyes. Many years had passed; I always had lots of questions and, now, sitting in front of me were four people who had lived it right along with me.

There was a quiet in the room when I asked about my father. Grandpa had a firm opinion about drinking. He knew he drank too much, and my father also drank too much. We were all thinking the same thing regarding how my father's choices had such a negative effect on all of us. As Grandpa talked, I could see the regret in his eyes. It was his son, after all. The conversation quickly turned to my mother, how she had wanted a little girl and how she loved me. "She got an infection," is what Grandma said.

As we talked about the past, there were sad moments when they described how I had to go live with my aunt and uncle after the car accident, followed by laughter when they talked about how they couldn't believe I painted that ole dog blue! As we talked, Grandma heard someone driving up the drive. She looked out the kitchen window, turned back to me wide-eyed, and said, "Sandy, it's your dad."

How did he know I was here? What was he going to be like? Should I be afraid? As I watched him pull up and get out of the car, the passenger side door also opened. Out came a little girl; she was maybe seven. Watching him walk closer to the door, my heart started racing. He was very tall, with dark hair that was mostly hidden by a baseball cap. As he entered the door, he had to duck so as not to hit his head. His bright green eyes caught mine. They quickly filled with tears, which he controlled by clearing his throat.

He had not had a shave in a few days and his skin was tan and weathered from the sun. Feeling a little awkward, I quickly shifted my eyes to the little girl. She had brown hair, about shoulder length, and green eyes that looked at me somewhat confused as to who I was.

I spoke only when asked a question.

"So you're fifteen?"

"Yes."

"Doing good in school?"

"Yes."

"I hear you're in the band?"

"Yup!"

"That's good. This is your half-sister."

"Hi," I said. The words just wouldn't come. I was shocked to see him. I had no memory of him. He had become like a fairy tale to me. I was an infant the last time he saw me. No one spoke. No one knew what else to say. As quickly as he came, he said, "I best be going." He turned around, walked back out the door, got into his car, and drove off. I turned back toward the dining room. Everyone was waiting to see what I would do. I looked at Grandma. She smiled at me and said, "I think he was curious to see you."

I was so unprepared for this. What would I have done differently if I had known? Would I have even wanted to see him? Why didn't I talk to him, ask the questions I wanted to know? I knew he had made some big mistakes in his life. Was I willing to forgive him for how he had messed up our family? I never had any anger toward him. All these years had passed, and now, the only thing I remember feeling for him as I watched him and my half-sister get back in the car and drive away was sadness.

That night as I talked to my parents about what had happened, I had such mixed emotions. Did I want my birth father to be a part of my life? How would that make my dad feel? My birth father wasn't there for me; my dad was. My birth father never came back for me. My dad had always been there. Ever since that Father's Day weekend when I first moved in with my parents, they were the ones who cared, the only mom and dad I ever knew. They were there when I needed a home, when I needed someone to love me and care for me, and when I needed someone to teach me. They were the steady influence in my life when I needed structure.

But I was still curious about my father. Did I want to open up that part of my life? There were too many uncertainties. I knew my parents would support me in any decision I made if I wanted to pursue a relationship with my father, but I wasn't willing to risk hurting my dad. So I made a decision—that day at my grandmother's house would be the last time I would ever again have contact with my birth father.

Sweet Sixteen

So many milestones happen at the age of sixteen. Soon I would be getting my license so I could drive myself to youth group. I would also be allowed to date, not that I had anyone particular in mind. I had other boyfriends in the past, nothing too serious. I wasn't allowed to date until I was sixteen, so most times it would be a crush here and there, but it wouldn't last for long. Our church was small enough that everyone knew everyone.

A week before my sixteenth birthday, I was sitting in the kitchen with my family. We enjoyed playing cards. Halfway through the game the phone rang. Mom was closest, so she answered. As she picked up the phone, she glanced my way. The call was for me, and she let everyone know it was a boy! Not being able to help themselves, my brothers teased me about getting the call as I tried to hear the voice on the other end of the receiver.

I wasn't expecting a call from a boy; I wondered who it was. "Hi, this is Eric from church." It wasn't hard for me to remember who Eric was. He always stood in the same place in the foyer just outside the sanctuary as he talked with his friends. Some mornings I would catch him smiling at me, so I would smile back. He had sent me a Christmas card the year before, and for the past several months, he came to find me each Sunday and sat with me during the service. Eric was always dressed in a nice suit. He had his own car and I would see him drive in and park each week before the service began. His car was easy to spot; it was an orange 1975 Mustang.

Eric knew from his friend that I wasn't allowed to date until I turned sixteen. Not wanting to wait too long, he asked if he could take me out to celebrate my birthday. As I turned toward my family who had been eagerly listening to the whole conversation, I asked

Mom and she reluctantly said, "Yes, just this once you can go." She had no idea that this was the start of something big and neither did I.

It was Saturday night, April 4, 1981. I was eagerly anticipating my first real date. I made sure everything was perfect. Eric was taking me to dinner at Red Lobster and then to Quaker Square to walk around the shops. Eric got to my house on time, as he said he would. The show *Hee Haw* was playing on the TV when Dad opened the front door. I wasn't ready yet, so the few minutes he had to wait on me were somewhat awkward. As I took the last of the hot rollers out of my hair, I could hear him talking to my parents. "Yes, dinner and I'll have her home by ten." Eric was reassuring them that he knew exactly what we were doing that night. By the look in his eyes as I entered the room, I could tell he was glad he didn't have to wait any longer.

Saying our goodbyes, we headed for the door. As we walked down the sidewalk to his car, I recognized it right away; it was the orange-and-black Mustang that he drove to church every Sunday morning. He opened the passenger side door and I got in. Sweet sixteen, how did I end up with someone so nice on my first date? I wasn't sure, but I wasn't complaining either.

I knew some things about Eric—he was older than me by three years, and he was attending college locally at the University of Akron studying mechanical engineering. He had a good job at Cope Pharmacy working in the pharmaceutical department. I knew he was very smart, and he was also very handsome.

I had always wanted to visit Quaker Square. It was the site of the original Quaker Oats factory in downtown Akron. The complex consisted of the former mill, factory, and silos. In the early 1970s it was turned into unique shops and restaurants. It was lit up beautifully at night, which made it a nice place to walk after dinner. One of the shops had an "Old Time Photo Booth." Thinking it would be fun to try, we agreed that next time we come we will get a picture made.

We continued to walk and talk until it was time for Eric to take me home. As we said our goodbyes, I knew there was something special about him. He was soft-spoken, kind of shy. We had a nice dinner, and he made a point to open all the doors for me. As we talked, I knew we had a lot in common. Even though he was older, we seemed to be comfortable with each other. I knew he had accepted Christ into his heart like I had. That was very important to me. I knew how Christ had changed my life, and if we went out on another date, I knew we would be sharing the stories of our pasts and our families, and for me, there was a lot to tell.

*****

The youth group at church was still a big part of my life. Every Sunday night, I was eager to go. Most of the time, my brother, Bruce, gave me a ride. There were at least twenty or so kids that attended. Bible study was important to me as God used this group to continue teaching me and growing me. I was no longer bored and shy like I had been at times during Sunday school, and I enjoyed learning and spending time with my friends.

Sunday evening, the day after my date with Eric, our Sunday night Bible study was coming to a close. I noticed my parents had slipped in the side door and were standing at the back of the room. As I looked back at them, Mom smiled and quickly motioned for me to turn around and pay attention. I was curious as to why they were there since Bruce usually drove me home when the study was over. I didn't know what they were up too.

After Stan finished our time by closing in prayer, the door from the hall opened and one of the parents came walking in carrying a large birthday cake. Everyone was in on the surprise and they all started singing "Happy Birthday." I couldn't believe that all of this was for me. I enjoyed my piece of cake as everyone congratulated me on being sweet sixteen. It had been a nice surprise from my parents, and I was very thankful.

*****

Green High School was only a few miles from my house. Although my daily bus ride was short, my goal now that I was sixteen was focused on getting my own car so I could drive myself. I started working at the local farmer's market, Green Farms, on Massillon Road. It was my first real job. I had done other things, like babysitting, but this was different. I worked the cash register, and when I wasn't doing that, I restocked the produce or worked behind the counter in the deli department.

The front of the store had large garage doors that opened so that the entire front of the store was open, making it easier to shop. These doors were always open when the store was open and were only closed in the fall and winter when the weather got cold. Eric would stop by from time to time to say hi. We had seen each other on and off at church, and we had attended some events with the kids from the youth group. I knew he really liked me, and I knew I would love to go out with him again. Unfortunately, I was not allowed. Mom had let us go out once for my birthday, but she didn't encourage us to see each other again. I wasn't sure why; Eric was a great guy!

The market was a popular place to visit. Attached to the market was a greenhouse. During the summer we sold flowers and plants, and in the fall a big truck full of pumpkins would stop by and the guys would unload them along with other decorative items, like corn stalks and bales of hay. During the Christmas season, another big truck would deliver live Christmas trees and wreaths, which made the whole place smell like we were in a forest.

Mom had to drop me off most of the time when I was scheduled to work. I usually found a ride home with one of the other girls. I remember being very sad during this time. I couldn't understand why I wasn't allowed to see Eric. As Mom dropped me off for work one morning, we hardly said a word to each other. She knew how I felt. As I got out of the car, she looked at me and said she loved me. I choked back the tears, shut the door behind me, and headed out to the barn behind the store. A shipment of cucumbers had just come in and I was helping to unpack and sort that day. I remember feeling glad that I didn't have to wait on customers. I really didn't feel like smiling, and I definitely didn't want to talk to anyone.

Red Mustang

The next day I had off work, I really wanted to learn to drive. I wanted my freedom, as most teenagers do. That way, I would be able to drive myself to work. Dad had been teaching me to drive. On the weekends he took me to my old grade school parking lot so I could practice. He drove around to the back, put the car in park, looked my way, and said, "Okay, are you ready for this?"

About that same time, I began taking driver's training at school. I didn't have the heart to tell Dad that, while driving the car during my class, I ran a red light. It had been raining that morning, and to tell you the truth, I was afraid I wouldn't be able to stop in time. Mom promised she wouldn't tell Dad that I had gotten an F for the day because of it. I wanted him to have confidence in me and my ability to be a safe driver. I eventually practiced enough and took the official driving test and passed. I worked hard at saving my money while looking for a car I could afford. Bruce had already owned several cars and had a red 1974 Mustang that he was trying to sell. I was anxious to get my own transportation and made a deal with him to buy the car for six hundred dollars. What did I know about buying a car? I only thought it was cute and it could get me where I needed to go, or at least it did for a little while.

It was a great feeling being able to go where I wanted when I wanted. No longer depending on Mom or Bruce for a ride, I could drive myself to youth group. I was able to spend more time hanging out with my friends each week, and it also meant I could go and see my grandmother whenever I wanted to.

*****

Mom was with me the day I wrecked my Mustang. She was sitting in the passenger seat as we were on our way to visit my grandmother. I was driving. I had been down that road many times. It was late in the afternoon, and the sun was glaring just enough so that I didn't see the car coming. I started to cross the road, but it was too late. The car coming the other way was now visible, but I was unable to stop in time. The other car smashed into the passenger side door, shattering the lower corner of the front windshield and spinning the car into the ditch.

"Mom, are you okay?"

She looked stunned. She had to get her bearings before she could speak. "I think I am," she said.

As I looked around me, I saw that other cars had stopped to help. The man from the car I hit was visibly shaken and upset. I got out of the car and walked to the closest house to call for help. By the time the police got there, Mom was sitting with the car door open and someone was asking her how she was. Neither Mom nor I needed an ambulance. The car was dented, and the windshield was broken, but I could still drive it. I was so thankful no one was hurt.

When I got home, all I could think of was how much I needed Eric. I knew he would be able to calm me down enough so we could come up with a plan on how to fix this mess I had gotten myself into. Before calling Eric though, I had to call my grandmother. By now, she must have been worried that we hadn't shown up. As I explained to her what happened, she got quiet. "Sandy," she said, "that's the same intersection where we had our accident when you were three!"

The next day I was still able to drive my car, and Eric asked if I could drive it over to his house so that he could take a look at it and see what he could do. I knew Eric enjoyed working on cars; he was good at it. One evening at a youth banquet at church, Eric was talking about painting his Mustang. He wanted to change the orange color and asked what color I thought would look nice. He smiled at me when I suggested the color metallic blue because that was the same color he was thinking of as well.

I was confident in Eric. I trusted him as he worked for weeks fixing the dents and painting the car. I knew it would never be the same; it had a lot of damage, but he did a great job making it look the best he could. As he worked on it, I would sit and talk with him for hours. That time we spent together brought us even closer than we were. I felt like he would do anything for me, and I was right.

I was glad to have my own car, now more than ever. Not only was I working as much as I could, but I planned to go to a new school in the fall. I had made a career choice to go into dentistry. A vocational school had been built a block from my high school, the Portage Lakes Joint Vocational School (JVS), and offered classes in diversified health fields. I was enrolled in the medical program and would attend my junior and senior years of high school, which proved to be a good decision for me.

The class was small, with only twelve girls. The curriculum consisted of both medical and dental. I think I surprised myself when I made the choice to go into dentistry. The fall of 1981 I began my studies within the Diversified Cooperative Health Occupations (DCHO) program with special interest in the dental field.

During my senior year, I participated in the cooperative education program, working as a chairside assistant for Dr. Gary Cortesi, DDS. I was seventeen and felt so fortunate to find an intern job where I could learn hands-on skills while finishing my education.

I had always been terrified of going to the dentist, but over the years, I began to learn more about it. I no longer had cavities, thanks to Blaine's wisdom when I was seven. Each day, I drove myself to class and enjoyed having the freedom to make some of my own decisions. God had blessed me. Many doors were opening, and I was getting excited about what the future would hold. I was voted DCHO class president my junior year and represented the school in the regional Job Interview Competition for Vocational Industrial Clubs of America. I was finally getting ahead. I was focused, and I knew what I wanted for my future, but still something was missing.

Eric was still on my mind. As much as I wanted to date him, I was obedient to my parents. I was told I had to wait a year before we could date again. During this time, I went out with other guys from the school, usually only once and only because Mom encouraged me to, but there was no one who compared to Eric. I knew I was in love, and it would be the longest year of my life. I often talked to Lori. She was still my best friend, and she knew Eric was waiting for me. Her encouraging words reminded me that "Eric must really love you for him to wait that long for you!" I knew she was right, and I think she also knew that hers and my dream of one day sharing an apartment was likely not going to happen…and so I waited.

The Gold Locket

Eric and I spent many hours talking on the phone. We weren't allowed to date, but we did get to see each other at church on the weekends and occasionally at the farmer's market when he would stop by when I was working. My brother Bruce, Eric, and I were all close in age. Sometimes Bruce and Eric got together on the weekends. I liked that because I got to see him when he came to the house to meet up with Bruce. Yes, Bruce intentionally did that so we could have a few moments together. One weekend I had been asked by one of the guys at school if I wanted to go see a movie. Tom and I had been friends for a while. We didn't share any classes together, but we had worked together on the yearbook. I had no intention of seeing someone on a serious level, since I knew that in a year I would be free to date Eric. I didn't go out much. Most of my time was spent with my friends from the youth group or with Lori, but this night it was just Tom and me.

The movie started early, so I was ready to go before I realized Eric was on his way to pick up Bruce. I had no idea what time he would get there, but I was hoping I had made my plans early enough because I didn't want to be leaving just as Eric was arriving. This could get awkward real fast.

As Tom arrived, he entered the front door much like Eric had on our first date on my birthday. Tom said hello to my mom and dad. I gathered my purse and started out the door. I thought, *Surely my parents would notice that Tom was a nice guy, but he was nothing like Eric.* As I made my way around Tom's silver Fiat X-19, I noticed the rust on the fenders and a large dent that went the length of the door frame. As I approached the passenger side, I thought Tom would have been right behind me. I glanced across the car to see him as he was opening the door on the driver's side. I could tell he was a little embarrassed as he signaled to me to come around so I could slide across the seat from his side. "That door doesn't work," he said. Glad that I had chosen to wear jeans that night, I walked to his side and proceeded to maneuver my way across the tiny seat and gear shift. I hoped he was a good driver so that I wouldn't have to exit the car for some emergency and thought to myself that maybe this was a bad idea.

Tom proceeded to back out of the driveway. I looked in the direction we were heading and saw the headlights of a car that had just turned the corner. As we started down the road, I could see it was a blue Mustang. Eric was on his way to get Bruce. I was hoping to be gone before he got there. I glanced at Eric as the cars passed going opposite directions. I couldn't help but look out the back window of the Fiat as Eric's blue Mustang turned into my driveway. I watched as long as I could. I know Eric saw me. I know we were both thinking the same thing—we would much rather be spending the evening together than apart.

That night at the movie, Tom sat quietly beside me. Occasionally his hand moved in the direction of mine, but before his hand ever got close to mine, I moved it out of his reach. I was polite as the movie came to an end and throughout the evening, but all I could think of was, *I will never do this again; it was too painful and not fair.*

Tom dropped me off after the movie. As I slid across the seat, I thanked him for a nice evening. I told him I would see him at school on Monday. He apologized for his car, which we laughed briefly about, and then we said goodbye. There was no doubt; I wanted to spend time with Eric, and now more than ever, I knew in my heart I didn't want him to see me drive off with anyone else ever again.

*****

My junior year of high school was a hard one. Eric and I talked all the time. Bruce would invite him over so we could briefly see each other. It was difficult, but I honored my parents' wishes and waited for the time when we could date. Eric sent me cards; there was never a holiday he missed. One evening around Valentine's Day, he had stopped by to go out with Bruce. In his hand was a gift. We were in the kitchen and no one was around. Eric pulled up a chair and sat beside me at the table. He handed me a small white box. Inside the box wrapped in white tissue paper was a gold heart locket. Inside the locket was a picture of Eric on one side and me on the other, and inscribed on the back was, "Love Eric." I was so surprised. I loved it. I wore that locket every day and looked forward to when we would be able to spend more time together.

Eric and I had gotten close that year of high school. I had shared with him my story of how my mother died when I was a baby and how I had been very sick and that I had lived with several family members before I was placed in the children's home and how eventually I went to live with the Pecks when I was seven.

My story wasn't one I talked about often, and to look at me, you would think I was just like any other girl my age. I had adjusted very well to my new life and family. Only by telling my story would anyone know of the journey I had been on. Eric was amazed when I told him my testimony and of how the Lord had revealed to me my past with the letter that was delivered to my uncle's house and how God had protected me through the years. He was also amazed that my maternal grandmother and paternal grandfather married. Who does that? I wanted him to meet my grandparents and see where I used to live. I had such clear memories and could describe for him in detail what had happened to me. He told me that he was already in love with me, but my testimony made him realize how God had his hand on me and it made him love me all the more.

I was excited for Eric to meet my grandparents and uncles. I had told them about Eric, and they already had lots of questions. Grandpa asked if Eric drank. Grandpa and his son, my birth father, had a past that affected our family, and for my father, it didn't end well. That was a major concern for my grandfather. I assured him that Eric was a great guy and that he loved me very much. I knew they would love Eric as much as I did, and I was right.

By my eighteenth birthday, Eric and I had waited the full amount of time that we were told we had to wait before we were allowed to date. Happy and eager to spend time together, we made plans to see each other every chance we got. We would go hiking on the weekends and out to dinner at night. We were excited to finally be able to do all the things we had talked about over the year we were apart. They say absence makes the heart grow fonder, and I think they were right. I had told myself, "If this is the Lord's will for my life, Eric will be there when the time comes," and he was.

*****

I was eager to introduce Eric to my grandparents and uncles. He and I had talked over the past year about how God had carefully woven my testimony into place, and I think he was eager to see the home where I used to live and meet the family I had talked so much about. I wasn't nervous for him to meet my grandparents—he already knew so much about them. I was more nervous about them meeting him. I knew they would love him, since my family loved me and wanted the best for me. I also knew my grandfather was hoping Eric was a good guy by *his* standards.

The day came when Eric and I drove together to Swinehart Road. The house was just as I had described. As we got out of the car, I could see Grandma looking from behind the tiny curtain that hung on the window on the kitchen door. I stepped out of the car onto the driveway and smiled at Eric. I was confident in everything that was about to happen. We entered the kitchen only to find a room full of people. My grandmother always invited everyone over when she knew I was coming. I think other members of the family were curious to see me after all the years I had been gone. We entered the room; all eyes were on us and no one said a word. "Hello, everyone; this is Eric!"

Grandma, who had been grinning the whole time, invited us to come in and have a seat. Each person shifted so everyone could fit into the tiny room. I introduced my family to Eric and tried to make light conversation. They were all studying him as if he was there to meet their approval. Grandpa, who had been sitting at the side of the room dressed in his bib overalls with his arms crossed in front, got up and put his hand out to shake Eric's. Uncle Billy, who had just come inside from the front porch after smoking his cigarette, tucked his half-smoked pack into his front shirt pocket and then also extended his hand to Eric and said hello. My uncle had served in the army. I had pictures of him in his uniform with my mom right before she died. He was young and proud to serve his country. Now years later, his health was failing, and he was frail and thin.

This was it. Finally, after a year, Eric was able to put faces to the names of the people who had had such an impact on my childhood. As I watched Eric with my family, I could tell they had an instant respect for him. Grandma quickly pulled out the bologna, bread, and chips and offered us a pop along with the tin of sugar cookies that always sat on the top of the microwave. Earlier in the day, Grandma had my other uncle, Bobby, run to the store to fetch some food for all the people she had invited for our visit.

Things hadn't changed much over the years; my grandparents were still poor, but their hearts were rich. I enjoyed watching everyone interact with Eric. As I looked around the room, I studied each person. Grandpa sat back in his seat after grabbing a plate of food, and again I watched painfully as he ate his sandwich and chips without his teeth. He occasionally interjected a comment or two to the story that was being told to be sure it was told correctly. Each person was eager to tell their version of the past. The conversation soon turned to laughter as one of my uncles chimed in and said, "Eric, have you heard about the time Sandy painted her dog blue?" Some stories never get old!

Eric taking me to my senior prom in his blue Mustang

Old Pictures and Worn-Out Books

I enjoyed the long talks I had with my grandmother. Some days it was just her and me sitting on her bed looking through old pictures and talking about the people in the photos. One afternoon as we talked, Grandma opened one of her dresser drawers and pulled out a small book. It was a bit dirty and worn, and the cover that was once white was now yellowed from age. "This was your mom's Bible," she said. I reached out and took it from her hand. So many things came to mind. I carefully opened it, randomly, toward the middle. It was a New Testament Red Letter Edition. I began to turn the pages. Each page was scattered with black and red words. I was a bit nervous; I didn't want to damage it. I didn't have any items that belonged to my mother, so seeing this was very special to me.

I continued to turn each page, hoping to find a personal note or an underlined verse or a bookmark—anything that would give me an idea what my mother believed about Jesus—but I found nothing. Surely, I missed something; my Bible has all kinds of notes and passages underlined where God had taught me or was teaching me, showing me His truth. I looked again but found nothing. Looking into my grandmother's eyes, I asked, "What did my mother believe?"

"She believed in Jesus," Grandma said. "She went to the church with the angel, where she's buried." Oh, how I wanted to believe that my mother was waiting for me in heaven. I hoped that she understood what it meant to have a personal relationship with Christ. My attention quickly turned to my grandmother, the one person who was sitting next to me, the one who was still with me. It was like she knew what I was going to say. She looked into my eyes and smiled and said, "Yes, Sandy, I believe."

Grandma gave me my mother's Bible. Over the years I have pulled it out to glance through it. We didn't have too many more conversations about my mother after that. I hoped that our conversation was true. Years later, I sat with my grandmother at her bedside the day before she died. I had since moved away, was married, and was living my own life raising my children. I came back to Ohio to see her one more time before she passed.

I prayed with her that day and told her I loved her. My hope is that someday I will meet my mother and see my grandmother again; much time will have passed. I can only imagine how we will sit and talk about the past and about all their grandchildren and their great-grandchildren. What a story I will have to tell then!

*****

The times I spent with my grandparents were precious. Talking to them helped me to understand not only the time frame of my earlier years but also the places I had been. The memories that God allowed me to retain were so very clear to me. It was confirmation of the story that I had shared with others about the little house with the long driveway and about family members whom I thought I would never see again.

I had such fond memories of Cambridge. I asked my grandmother about it. She mentioned how my aunt and uncle lived close to where the old farmhouse still stood. The previous owners had since passed away and new owners had moved in. She asked me if I would like to take a trip to see it and to see my Aunt Carol and Uncle Gary, to which I eagerly agreed, so we planned a weekend to visit Cambridge.

Aunt Carol and Uncle Gary lived in a trailer. My uncle had built an addition on to it to make it bigger. They were happy for us to come for a visit. After about an hour-and-a-half drive, we approached their home. I could see the driveway beautifully lined with black-eyed Susans. Several pink plastic flamingos were placed here and there throughout the yard, which brought back memories of the garden my aunt had years ago. Grandma, Uncle Bobby, Uncle Billy, and I got out of the car and started for the door. Before we got up the walk, my aunt pushed open the screen and came out with her arms open wide. Bypassing my uncle, who was in front of me, she reached out and hugged me tight. I had grown since she had seen me last. I no longer had an eating disorder, and I was several inches taller than she was.

Still holding me by my shoulders, she stepped back to look at me. Aunt Carol hadn't changed much. Her voice was still the same. I hadn't noticed before that day how her nose would wrinkle up as she smiled, in a cute way. Her hair was now brown, and much shorter. For the most part, she was just as I had remembered her, and she was very excited to see us.

She welcomed us in as Uncle Gary came around the side of the house. He had been working in the barn out back of the house and saw us drive up. He hadn't changed much either. He still wore his cowboy boots. His hair was still slicked back on the sides, just like I remembered, but his sideburns were now gray. On his eyes he sported a pair of aviators, which he quickly removed as he approached us. His eyes were still as blue, and he winked at me just like he used to when I was four.

That evening we sat in the living room and talked until it was late. Tomorrow we would go sightseeing around town. I was curious to see the farmhouse and the barn where I had so much fun during the summers when I was four and five. I was tired, so Aunt Carol showed Grandma and me to a small bedroom that was just off the dining room.

Grandma and I shared a room that weekend. I hadn't been that close to her since I was little. I sensed she wanted to treat me as if I were still her little granddaughter, like I was when I was three. She wanted to do everything for me, making sure I was comfortable. I appreciated what she was trying to do, so I let her. She knew I was now old enough and could take care of myself. She had missed out on all my childhood, but I wasn't her little granddaughter anymore.

Those years were long gone. I was now eighteen and able to care for myself.

Our relationship was different now, but the love my grandmother had for me was just as strong as it was all those years ago. My mother would not have been disappointed in her. Grandma did all she could to take care of me. I had been taken out of her hands, but it all happened the way God planned. She had not let my mother down when she promised her she would take care of me. She did the best she could, and I reassured her of that. As we sat in the stillness of that small bedroom, just the two of us, we looked forward to a new season in our lives. We knew that after all that had happened to us over the years, it was all going to be okay.

As the years have passed by, my grandmother is now gone. I wish I could sit with her one more time and ask just one more question. I think we all have those moments when we think to ourselves, *If I had only asked about this, if I had only had more confidence, if I had only spent more time, if only...*

*****

It had been thirteen years since I had last been to Cambridge. The air was different. Some of the local farms had since stopped growing corn, so most of the fields were bare. A few of the farmers still had cattle and chickens, and occasionally the memory from years gone by of a rooster crowing would be reignited by the distant sounds around us. As we drove down the road to the house where I had such fond memories, it was no longer dirt like it used to be. It had been paved years prior.

I wish I would have had the nerve to knock on the farmhouse door to let the new owners know how I used to love visiting their property, but I wasn't brave enough to do that. We pulled the car off to the side and got out. I hiked to the top of the hill that was across the street from the house that held so many memories. The field no longer had corn growing, and I'm not sure if anything at all was planted. We stopped for a short time, long enough to get a few pictures and to reminisce.

What a gift I had been given; I was so thankful to God. His blessings on my life hadn't stopped when He revealed my past by allowing me to find my family. God continued to bless me as I revisited my memories and my loved ones, and I am thankful that He did. As I glanced their way, my Aunt Carol and Uncle Gary were enjoying watching me. I could tell that the memories were flooding back for them as well. God had been taking care of me since I left their care. Now that I was eighteen, I had dreams of my own for my future and who I wanted to build a life with. I was growing up and would soon be making my own decisions.

My visit to the farm house in Cambridge when I was eighteen

Aunt Carol and Uncle Gary the day we spent visiting Cambridge when I was eighteen

Gunne Sax and White Dresses

Our engagement photo.
Notice the gold locket!

Eric and I were growing closer as the year went on. We had talked about the future and about marriage. I knew he had been looking at rings, but there were certain goals that we wanted to attain before we could move on with the next step of our relationship.

I had just graduated from high school and the DCHO pro-gram, and I had already begun working full-time at the office of Joe Hale III, DDS, as his dental assistant. Eric was still in college working on his degree in engineering while at the same time working as a co-op engineer at Goodyear Aerospace. We knew money would be tight until he could graduate and work full-time as a mechanical engineer, but we knew we could do it.

We had planned to go to dinner later that week to a very elegant restaurant in Stow called the Silver Pheasant. I had never been to such a fancy restaurant before, so I thought to myself, *This is the night that he's going to ask me to marry him!*

It was a warm Saturday in June of 1983. It was a beautiful day, so we decided to go hiking at the Gorge, a local park in Cuyahoga Falls that was part of the metro park system. The park had great hiking trails and caves that we liked to explore, along with waterfalls and an occasional deer.

Eric picked me up at my house in his blue Mustang and we drove to the park. It was before noon, and we knew it would begin to get hot in the early afternoon. I was enjoying the day, spending time with Eric. After all, this was what I had waited for. I eagerly anticipated the night when I thought for sure he was going to ask me to be his wife during a beautiful candlelight dinner at an elegant restaurant. I even knew what I was going to wear, and in my mind, I had it all figured out.

We had already hiked for at least an hour when we stopped at the base of the biggest waterfall. Large rocks lined the banks, and we were able to sit on them as we took a break before heading back to the car.

Eric seemed quiet. I remember smiling at him and I wondered what he was thinking. After a minute he looked at me and began talking about our future. He reached into his jeans pocket and turned it inside out. Attached to the inside of his pocket by a safety pin was a gold diamond ring. Getting down on one knee, he loosened the ring from the safety pin and held it for me to see. Afraid he would somehow lose the ring while hiking, he made sure he didn't by firmly attaching it inside his pocket.

He smiled at me, and I acknowledged his cleverness. He said he loved me and wanted to know if I would marry him. I was totally thrown off by his timing, which is exactly what he was wanting. Thinking he would ask me later that week at dinner, I was definitely surprised. "Yes, of course!" I said.

As he slid the ring on my finger, he asked, "Are you sure you want to marry me? Because this is it!"

How could he have any doubts? "Of course, I want to marry you!" I said. I had known that for some time.

We were excited to tell our families. My dad was playing in a baseball game not far from where we were, but before we would go to his game to tell everyone the good news, we realized we were starving. The closest fast-food restaurant we could find was a place called the Red Barn. How romantic to go get burgers and fries to celebrate our engagement. The food was awful. We laughed about it as we finished our meal. I knew that later that week we would officially celebrate with a beautiful meal in a fancy restaurant, but what made me the happiest was just spending time together, whether it was burgers or otherwise. We were together, and to me that was what was most important.

*****

The Silver Pheasant restaurant was the perfect place to celebrate our engagement. As we entered the dining room, we were escorted to our table, where we enjoyed our meal. I wanted to look my best, so I wore the dress that I had planned to wear; it was a Gunne Sax dress that Eric had bought for me. It was a beautiful champagne color, and my gold locket looked nice with it. As we enjoyed our evening, we began talking about what date would be best for the wedding, so we set our sights on the following summer. It would give us time to do all the things that needed to be done.

We knew we wanted to have the wedding at Manchester Trinity Chapel, which was a special place for us. It was where we met, where I came to Christ, and where we still attended every Sunday. All our friends, who knew all along that we would someday get married, would want to attend. I would ask Lori to be my maid of honor, and Eric wanted to ask his brother-in-law, Jerry, to be his best man. We were close to Eric's sister, Cheryl, her husband, Jerry, and their two daughters, Christina and Elizabeth, who we both thought would be wonderful flower girls. The date was set for Saturday, June 2, 1984.

Me with Christina and Elizabeth, my soon-to-be nieces and flower girls

I had no idea how much planning it took, but I soon learned. Mom knew it was going to be a busy year, and looking back on it now, I realize how much work she did to make our day special. As the months seemed to fly by, I had not found a dress yet. I wasn't sure what kind of dress I wanted. I had been a bridesmaid for a few of my girlfriends that got married the summer after graduation, but looking for my wedding dress was different.

Mom knew a few shops to start our search, so we planned a Saturday morning to try on gowns. The bridal dress shop Mom and I visited was an older store, not very big, with ornate white and ivory gowns on white hangers that were hung around every corner. Large crystal chandeliers, which created a warm glow in the shop, hung in the center of the ceiling of every room. The walls of the shop had been covered with a beautiful pink and white velvet embossed paper. Each of the rooms had platforms to stand on, and there were many mirrors, which made it easier to see the gowns when I tried them on.

Passing rows and rows of dresses, we were escorted to the back of the shop. The saleslady asked me what I had in mind. I didn't know. I had no idea what would look good on me. One of my friends had worn a very puffy dress for her wedding. I knew I wasn't a fan of the big sleeves and long train, so with that information, the saleslady began her quest to find a dress that was to my liking and to Mom's budget.

Dress after dress I tried on; they were either too ornate, not ornate enough, or the wrong color. I really wanted a white dress. The color of the dress was important to me because Eric and I had been faithful in keeping our promise to honor each other and our faith before marriage.

We had been at the shop for quite a while and I hadn't found a dress that I liked, and I was getting tired. Mom and the saleslady seemed to be running out of ideas. The lady was very kind, but occasionally she would look up at me over the top of her glasses and sigh. I was ready to call it quits for the day when, while contemplating the last dress I had on, I twirled around on the elevated platform to give the dress one more glance. As I looked at myself in the trifold mirror, the reflection of a dress that was hanging in the very back of the room caught my eye. I turned around and wondered why I hadn't seen it an hour ago. I would like to say I heard a chorus of angels singing at the sight of it, but it felt like I had. Before I even had a chance to try it on, I knew it was the one.

The saleslady was more than happy to retrieve the dress and announce with a smile on her face that the dress may not have to be altered because it was already my size. I slipped the dress over my head; the fabric was soft and seemed to slide right into place. The neckline was beautiful, and the long sleeves and smaller train seemed to be just the look that was best for me. I was comfortable, and I felt pretty. This was it. I knew this was the one. The style, the fit, the color, the only thing left now was the price. As Mom looked at the price tag, she smiled and said, "Okay, this is good!" I felt like the dress had been quietly waiting for me as it hung by itself on the door frame. The dress that I would wear on my wedding day would be special to me, as I would wear it when I say my sacred vows to Eric in the presence of our friends, family, and God. This dress had to be perfect, and to me it was.

Me wearing my "perfect" dress

We were to meet with Reverend Carse that night. Eric and I were counseling with him before the wedding. Reverend Carse was Blaine and Terri's pastor. He was very kind and had asked us some very hard and thought-provoking questions during our sessions with him.

Eric and I had told him how we had been unable to date and how our relationship had grown stronger through it. We talked about our testimonies and what the Lord meant to each of us. We only had a few more meetings and then our counseling sessions would be complete.

Mom and I had to get home because Eric would be at the house soon and I had to get ready for our next meeting. I still wanted to get a bite to eat. The saleslady gave us a date when we could pick up the dress. She said she would have it ready for me after she was able to steam it to remove the wrinkles. I looked forward to the day when I could wear my beautiful white dress.

*****

Planning our wedding would be a very busy time for everyone. Invitations, bridesmaid's dresses, food…the list goes on and on. The bridesmaids would wear lavender-colored dresses, and the men would wear gray-colored tuxedos. Eric and I would both be in white. We were trying to save money where we could, and Mom had lots of ideas. She was a good seamstress. She had made her wedding dress, which always fascinated me, and even though I wasn't much interested in sewing myself, I always admired how she could put together an outfit.

Mom and Granny Kmetz made the bridesmaid's dresses and my veil. Mom had also done work as an interior decorator and had an eye for arranging flowers. I would sometimes go with her during the summer, when I was on break from school, to the large warehouse where she would buy her dried and silk flowers at wholesale prices. I would explore the large building while she shopped. Rows and rows of metal shelves were stocked with every kind of flower imaginable. Now that she was planning on making the arrangements for the wedding, she would have to revisit the warehouse once again. We would need flowers for the wedding party, for decorating the sanctuary, and for decorating the fellowship hall where we planned on having the reception.

We had so much to do, and Mom and Granny Kmetz did much of the work. The food was going to be ham sandwiches and Granny's potato salad served buffet style along with other homemade goodies. We chose a cake with three tiers, white with lavender-colored flowers. A working fountain was set at the base of the cake, and it had a small light under it that lit up the cake beautifully. I am thankful to the ladies of our church who graciously served at the reception. As I look back, I remember how blessed we were to be involved with a church that was so giving.

Granny was always supportive and encouraging. I had talked to her occasionally about Eric and how much he meant to me. We had spent some time talking during one of the summers when we had shared a bedroom on vacation at Holden Beach. She was happy for us. She loved Eric and knew that he made me happy. She knew he was smart, and she also knew he would take good care of me. She sent me a beautiful handmade note the summer we got engaged. I have the note to this day; it reads as follows:

7-14-1983
My Dear Granddaughter,

Congratulations on your engagement. May the Lord bless it and give you the wisdom for a future bride. May I help with the planning? I love you and Eric, and if this is what you both want, praise the Lord.

Grandma

I was grateful for my grandma's blessing, not only hers but my other grandmas' as well. Grandma Cole and Grandma Peck were all looking forward to the June wedding as we all continued to make our plans for the next year.

Are You Sure?

During the year of preparations, we had made a decision on where we would live after the wedding. Eric's parents owned a duplex that was located on East Avenue in Akron. It would be close to the university and I would be able to take the freeway to get to work at Doctor Hale's office. Our first home; it was perfect for us. We had bought second-hand furniture for the living room. Our coffee table was an old door that Eric's brother had made into a table by attaching four wooden legs to it. We were able to purchase a new dining room table from money that had been given to us by Eric's parents. After we spent a week of honeymooning in the Pocono Mountains, our home would be ready for us.

June 1st was here before we knew it—Friday night, the night before the big day. After rehearsal at the church, everyone drove a few miles down the road to Eric's parents' house for dinner. We were surrounded by friends and family, and as everyone gathered to fill their plates, Reverend Carse blessed the meal. I was so nervous I don't recall eating much as we mingled with our loved ones. Christina and Elizabeth, who were only three and five at the time, were so excited for the next day when they could wear their flower girl dresses. Cheryl had made them, and the girls looked adorable. It seemed everything was now moving so fast.

Lori, my maid of honor, had been such a support to Eric and me. We had been best friends since I was seven. We were so little then and had talked for years about our dreams and what we would do when we grew up. I glanced her way. She saw me looking at her and smiled back. I was happy that she was there to stand beside me the next day, and I know she was too.

After dinner was over, Eric and I said goodbye to our friends and family and then helped clean up the kitchen. It was getting late. Even though I was tired, I knew I wouldn't be able to sleep. I had too many thoughts swirling around in my mind. Eric drove me home and we said our goodbyes. Tomorrow was a big day, and we both agreed on how we looked forward to spending a week away...just the two of us.

*****

The cool morning air filled my room. I had left the windows open during the night. The soft breeze brought with it the smell of flowers that were blooming just outside. The birds were just beginning to sing. I looked at the alarm clock on my nightstand and realized it was still early. I hadn't slept much during the night; this was the last night I would spend at my parents' house before I became Eric's wife.

Today was finally here. The last thing a bride wants during her wedding is to have something go wrong. I had tossed and turned as my mind reviewed each detail of the ceremony. Now that it was morning, I figured if I couldn't sleep anyway, I might as well get up and enjoy a cup of coffee.

I slipped on my slippers and shuffled down the hall to the bathroom. The sun was just beginning to rise. No one was up yet, and the house was still dark. I flipped on the light and stood in front of the large mirror that covered the wall in front of me. My hair, which was shoulder length, was messy from my tossing and turning during the night. As I moved my bangs off my forehead with the swipe of my hand, I squinted to adjust my eyes to the light. My reflection was a little blurry. I rubbed my eyes a few more times and was finally able to focus. Now able to see, I couldn't believe the change that had taken place over night. "This can't be!" A red bump had formed right in the middle of my chin—a pimple. It wasn't there yesterday. Just the day before I looked fine! This was not what I wanted to deal with on the day of my wedding.

Ironically, a conversation I had the week before with the girls that I worked with in the dental office came to mind. We were discussing the upcoming nuptials when one of the girls said, "I am so excited for you. I know you will make a beautiful bride. I sure hope your face doesn't break out or something. That would be awful!" I jokingly smiled back at her and laughed while trying to make light of the uncomfortable comment. The more that I thought about what she had said, the more I worried that it might happen. What if it did?

As I remembered that conversation, I couldn't help but laugh to myself as I thought, *If this is the worst thing that can go wrong today, I'll be okay.* Still standing in the bathroom, I reached out and opened the drawer where I kept my makeup. I pulled out my tube of Maybelline concealer and casually tossed it on the counter, knowing that I would want to use it later when Lori and the other girls came to the house to help me get ready for the ceremony.

By now, I was more awake than ever. I could hear Mom, who was now up and in the kitchen, clanking the pots and pans as she prepared to make breakfast. The smell of coffee was beginning to fill the house as it was brewing. It was a comforting smell. The smell of coffee reminded me of the time that I had spent when I was admitted to the children's home clinic during the two weeks when I was dealing with my eating disorder. I had come a long way since then. I was now healthy and strong. I no longer needed counseling. Years ago, my world had changed for the better when I began living with the Pecks. I had adjusted well.

As I stood looking at myself in the mirror, I thought, *Today I am starting a new chapter in my life*, and it felt right. I was ready. Flipping off the bathroom light, I realized that the wedding was now less than twelve hours away. Smiling, I shuffled off to the kitchen to have breakfast with Mom and to pour myself that big wonderful cup of coffee.

Mom had made us girls lunch that afternoon. We all decided to meet at my house before we drove together to the church. Lisa, who was Eric's younger sister, Cathy, Jill, and, of course, Lori all spent the afternoon with me as we prepared for the wedding that would take place at the church later that evening. Mom had us pose for a picture as we stood in the driveway about to leave with boxes of things for the reception and our makeup kits in hand. It was now less than three hours until my dad would walk me down the aisle and give me away to the man I would spend the rest of my life with.

I was grateful to my friends and especially Lori. Jill and I had met at church. We were both involved in the youth group and music ministry. Eric and Jill had gone to the same high school and had dated at one time. Even though they had, I didn't mind. Jill was a close friend. She was supportive of Eric and me, and I couldn't imagine her not being a part of our special day. Cathy and I had met at the vocational school. We had been in the same medical class together our junior and senior years. Lisa and I grew close during our time together in the youth group and when I spent time at her house visiting Eric.

Once we arrived at the church, the girls and I were escorted to a room in the back of the sanctuary. The room was where the youth group often met on Sunday night. Several of the ladies at the church had set it up for us with mirrors and tables so all of us girls could get ready. Mom, who had driven separately, was now dressed in her long purple gown. The color of her dress coordinated beautifully with the colors of the wedding party. In her hands was a box of flowers. She put the final touches on each bouquet as she handed them to the girls. The room was now full of color. Mom had done a good job; not only were the flowers beautiful, but Mom was too.

I was now starting to get nervous. Lori saw I was a bit anxious, so she started talking to me about all that had led up to this day. How thankful I was to have her. Of all my friends, she was the one who knew me best. As Lori and I talked, in came my three grandmothers. They were enjoying visiting with each other. Each one was dressed in her finest dress. They all looked so elegant. They each approached me and smiled as they took turns complimenting me on my dress. What a blessing it was to have all of them there. Grandma Cole, with tears in her eyes, took me by the hand and smiled. She never thought she would ever see me again and now here she was just moments from seeing me walk down the aisle on my wedding day. She hugged me and gave me a kiss and said she would see me later.

Lori helped me with my dress. Together, we slipped it up over my head and pulled it down around me. Mom had embellished the dress by sewing on a layer of beautiful white lace around the bottom. As the dress fell into place, it looked and felt perfect, just like it did that day in the boutique when Mom and I picked it out. The veil Mom had made for me was a wreath of flowers and soft tulle. As Mom placed the veil on my head, she pulled the tulle up and over my face. Standing in front of the mirror, I finally saw the completed look. I could see my friends, who were standing behind me, watch as Mom lifted the bell of the dress to straighten it. The final touches were now complete. Mom handed me my bouquet, and it was time.

The sanctuary lights were dimmed, and the candles were lit. I was dressed and ready to go. Mom hugged me and reminded me to hold the bouquet straight. Then she smiled and left the room. Now it was just the girls and me. As we walked to the foyer and stood behind the closed double doors that led to the sanctuary, Dad greeted me and told me I looked beautiful. He took me by the arm and turned to walk with me down the aisle. As we stood there waiting, my mind drifted to the conversation Eric and I had the day he proposed to me at the park. He had knelt down on one knee and asked me if I would marry him and then he asked, "Are you sure?"

The music in the sanctuary became quiet as I stood there waiting for my time to enter. If there was one thing I knew in my heart to be true, it was, "Yes, Eric, I'm sure. I want to marry you!"

From This Day Forward

I was told by other brides that they couldn't remember anything about their wedding day. It had gone by so fast that the details had become vague over time. As I stood in the church foyer, I told myself that I would walk slowly with my dad so that I would remember everything.

I had asked Terri if she would do the music for the ceremony. She had a beautiful solo voice, and I had enjoyed singing with her during special occasions at church. Eric and I were so happy when she agreed to sing the songs we had picked out that were special to us. As she sang the last song, it was now time for me to walk down the aisle.

Dad looked at me and smiled. He was so handsome in his gray tuxedo. I held onto his arm tightly as the last of the bridesmaids walked to the front of the sanctuary. Cheryl positioned Christina and Elizabeth while they awaited their turn. They were carrying baskets filled with white flower petals that they were to drop on the white runner as they walked down the aisle. They were so young, and they looked so sweet in their lavender dresses. Cheryl and Jerry had talked to them about what they were supposed to do. We hoped they would be okay walking down the aisle by themselves.

Sheepishly, side by side, the girls passed by all the wedding guests who were smiling and making comments to each other about how cute they were. Lisa, who was also their aunt, had already walked the aisle and was waiting for them at the front. She smiled at Christina and Elizabeth. Their dad, Jerry, was standing just a few feet away from them as Eric's best man. He motioned for them to take their Aunt Lisa's hand so she could direct them to where they were to stand. She was the familiar face they needed to reassure them that they were doing a good job.

As the double doors to the sanctuary opened, I stepped forward. Mrs. Coleman, the church's music director, began to play the "Bridal Chorus" on the organ. I took a deep breath and intentionally didn't move. At the sound of the music, everyone stood up and turned to look my way. I wanted to remember, even if it was for just a moment, exactly how everything looked.

Lori, Lisa, Cathy, and Jill all stood facing my way. I looked at each one and was thankful for such good friends. Christina and Elizabeth, although fidgety, stopped to see what was going on when the music suddenly changed. There were four groomsmen—Scott, Mike, Jerry, and Bruce. Scott and Mike had known Eric from high school and college. Jerry was Cheryl's husband and the best man. Eric and I looked up to Jerry and Cheryl; we had many good conversations with them, and we loved spending time with their daughters, our nieces, Christina and Elizabeth. And then there was my brother, Bruce. He had been such an encouragement to Eric and me, and I was glad to see him there.

I looked out across the room; most of the pews were full. Waiting for me at the front of the room was Eric. He was standing, dressed in his white tux, smiling at me. The lights had been dimmed low except for the lights directly above the altar. A large white arch stood at the center of the platform. Mom had decorated it with white flowers and candles on each side. Behind the altar was the colorful stained glass. Many Sundays I had studied that glass as I sat listening to the Sunday's message, and now, just moments away, I would stand before it and say my vows.

My heart was racing as I took a step forward. Dad, who was well on his way, was almost a step ahead of me. I tugged lightly on his arm to slow him down. I wanted this moment to last. I wanted to look at the faces of the people standing up for me as I walked by.

Stan and Joyce, my youth leaders, were two of the first people I saw. God had placed them in my life during my middle school and high school years. I had grown so much during that time. They were encouraging and supportive, and because of their teaching, I had learned and grown in my understanding of the Bible.

As I continued down the aisle, I glanced from side to side and smiled at the many faces of our friends and relatives. Many of these people knew me since I was seven years old, after I had begun living with the Pecks. I was happy to see Aunt Carol, Uncle Gary, Kenny, Terry, Uncle Billy, and Uncle Bobby. I had come a long way from the days of temper tantrums and eating issues. I was thankful that God had given me this day to celebrate with them.

Slowly, I continued to walk as I approached the front of the sanctuary. The first two pews were where our closest family members had been seated. I was happy that I had all three of my grandmothers there with me—Grandma Peck, Granny Kmetz, and Grandma Cole. I knew they loved and supported me, and I knew they loved Eric and were happy for us.

I thought about the time I had spent with them growing up; many precious memories came flooding back to my mind. I remembered sitting in the beautiful ornate church on Sunday morning with Grandma Peck and how she proudly introduced me as her grand-daughter. I thought back on how I enjoyed the long talks I had with Granny Kmetz on those summer vacations at the beach house and how she made lemon water for me when I was sick. And then there was Grandma Cole. I had less than five years with her since we found each other when I was fourteen. For me it was a lifetime of memories that we had shared in such a short time. How thankful I was to have her in my life. I was never supposed to see her again, but God had other plans. I was grateful for my three brothers. They had stood with me at this very altar when I prayed to invite Jesus into my heart.

Dad and I walked arm in arm. My dad, the dad *I adopted* the day after Father's Day. I have heard a saying that says, "Anyone can be a father, but it takes someone special to be a daddy." That's what God gave me—a special daddy! He was the dad who took all those little girls from the children's home out for ice cream, the dad who took me in and cared for me and who has never let me down. That's my dad!

I felt so beautiful in my white dress, the one Mom and I picked out together, like I did the first Christmas I spent with my family when Mom had made her and me matching dresses. That first Christmas when I was seven, Mom had baked and decorated and created a home that, at that time, was foreign to me. She showed me what it was like to have a mommy and what it took to be a mommy. Mom had encouraged me with scripture the day I was reunited with my Grandma Cole. I had never seen someone reading their Bible early in the morning before the day started, but many days I saw her. I never knew my birth mom, but I am thankful each day for my mom. She was tough, but at times she had to be. She never gave up on me.

Here we were all together in one place. I was surrounded by the important people in my life that had made such a difference in me along the way. Dad and I continued our walk down the aisle. I looked around the room; this sanctuary held many years of special memories for me, defining moments that had shaped my way of thinking. In this room I was confronted with choices and decisions that I had to make that had shaped my destiny for all eternity. I was grateful for such a place and grateful for those in my life that cared for me when I couldn't care for myself. I was blessed, and I didn't want to take any of it for granted. I looked up at Eric, who was standing at the altar, patiently waiting on me, patiently waiting like he had been all along. No more waiting, now it was time.

Where would I be if God had not divinely orchestrated my life? Everything I had gone through in my nineteen years had brought me to the place where I was now. Standing at the altar, I was ready to commit my life to being a wife, and hopefully, someday a mother. I knew that if God could take care of me through all the past, then there was no reason to worry; I had nothing to fear.

I took a deep breath and reached out for Eric's hand. We smiled at each other as we turned to face the beautiful stained-glass windows. Reverend Carse began the ceremony and a sense of calmness came over me, and at that moment I prayed. "Lord, every step of my life, when I couldn't understand my circumstances, you never left me alone. When I prayed and asked for your help, you heard me. I have learned because you have taught me. How valuable and precious I am in your eyes, and I am thankful to you, Lord, for loving me."

Mom adding the finishing touches

Dad walking me down the aisle

*Saying our vows, June 2,
1984, before the beautiful
stained-glass windows*

My family

Phyllis Jean Sharp Cole

Sandra Jean Cole Peck Gamble

Consider the ravens, for they neither sow nor reap; they
have no storeroom nor barn, and yet God feeds them;
how much more valuable you are than the birds!
—Luke 12:24 (NASB)

Not the End

Many years have passed since our wedding day. Eric is still the love of my life. We were so young back then when we got married, and over time we have grown even closer together. God has blessed us with our two children, Benjamin and Adam, and now our grand-children. I'm thankful that when my boys were younger, I was able to stay home with them, which also allowed me the time to serve in several ministries.

Eric and the boys have continued to be patient with me. I have made many mistakes since my wedding day when I was nineteen, and I have learned many things about myself. Over time, God has continued to work on my heart to teach me as Eric and I raised our boys. Serving within our church and the community, I found that I enjoyed investing my time mentoring in ministries that involved chil-dren, teen moms, young married moms, and moms facing unwanted pregnancies.

As I was encouraged to write my story, I knew my life was not about chance or luck. It happened just the way it should have. Many times, I have heard how tapestries can relate to our own lives as believers in Christ. This analogy is so true. Tapestries are wall hang-ings, usually very ornate, made from many threads of fabric woven together over time. Some threads are dark and some are vivid in color. It takes a skilled master weaver to create such beauty.

If you have ever watched a tapestry being made, you would notice that the master weaver uses the appropriate colored thread at the appropriate time. Gradually, and with great patience, he creates a pictorial that beautifully portrays a story.

Sometimes, as you look at the cloth, you can tend to focus only on the underside of the fabric where the warped threads are…it isn't so pretty. When going through life's difficulties, at times we only see the loose threads and unmatched colors. With God's help, he changed my perspective.

As I have written these pages, I can see the comparison as it relates to my own life. The threads of my story have slowly come together. I have remembered details from conversations held years ago and realized that these memories were beginning to fade. The few photos I have gathered over time have not only confirmed the past but have also added light to long-forgotten memories. These threads, whether dark or vivid, are all I had until the Master Weaver presented my woven design, my beautiful pictorial.

Each of our lives can resemble a tapestry. Dark threads intertwined with beautiful colors. But if we only look at the backside where the warped and the weft threads are visible, we can get discouraged. There will always be trials, hardships, and tears; but there will also be moments of great joy, hope, and happiness. Don't forget to look at the other side. To my family, and others, as you read my story, remember that God has a plan for you. Trust Him; you may not know what His will is at the time, but rest in this assurance: He does.

For He established a testimony in Jacob
And appointed a law in Israel,
Which He commanded our fathers
That they should teach them to their children,
That the generation to come might know,
even the children *yet* to be born,
That they may arise and tell *them* to their children,
That they should put their confidence in God
And not forget the works of God,
But keep His commandment.

—Psalm 78:5–7 (NASB)

The Weaver

My life is but a weaving
Between my God and me.
I cannot choose the colors
He weaveth steadily.

Oft' times He weaveth sorrow;
And I in foolish pride
Forget He sees the upper
And I the underside.

Not 'til the loom is silent
And the shuttles cease to fly
Will God unroll the canvas
And reveal the reason why.

The dark threads are as needful
In the weaver's skillful hand
As the threads of gold and silver
In the pattern He has planned.

He knows, He loves, He cares;
Nothing this truth can dim.
He gives the very best to those
Who leave the choice to Him.

Grant Colfax Tullar

About the Author

First-time author, Sandy Gamble, didn't realize the impact her life story could have on children and families of adoption and foster care.

Before she was five years old, Sandy experienced one tragedy after another. These events led to her being placed in the care of Summit County Children's Services for treatment of eating and behavioral disorders.

Sandy met her husband at an early age. They were married when she was nineteen and have been together for over thirty-six years.

She studied to become a dental assistant in her home state of Ohio and worked until she and her husband moved to Florida. When their two sons were young, Sandy was a stay-at-home wife and mother. Throughout the years, Sandy invested her time in many different ministries within her church and community. She served on staff at her church as the director of Children's Ministries and counseled moms in crisis through First Care Pregnancy Center and Hannah's Home of South Florida. Discipling, teaching, and counseling unwed moms and teen moms became her passion.

Sandy's story is an amazing one of God's provision throughout her life. Even as an infant, God had his hand on her, protecting and guiding her along the way. Sandy's story is a testimony that miracles do happen. Don't lose faith. There is always hope in every situation. Even when we don't understand why, trust God; He has a plan!

CPSIA information can be obtained
at www.ICGtesting.com
Printed in the USA
LVHW020313201021
700930LV00002B/227